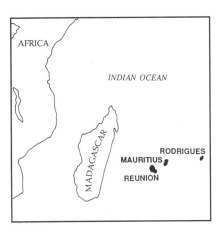

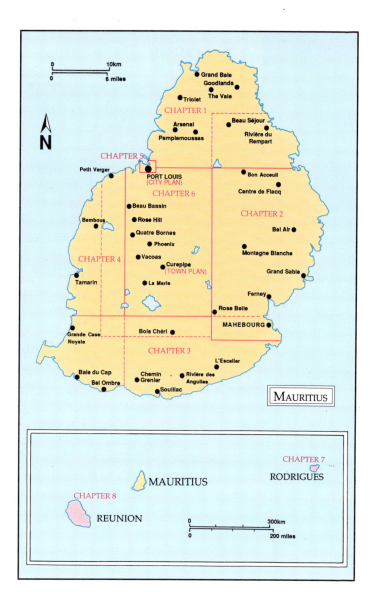

VISITOR'S GUIDE
MAURITIUS
RODRIGUES & REUNION

KATERINA & ERIC ROBERTS

MPC
HUNTER

Published by:
Moorland Publishing Co Ltd,
Moor Farm Road West,
Ashbourne,
Derbyshire DE6 1HD
England

ISBN 0 86190 437 0

Published in the USA by:
Hunter Publishing Inc,
300 Raritan Center Parkway,
CN 94, Edison, NJ 08818
ISBN 1 55650 527 2 (USA)

© Katerina & Eric Roberts 1992

All rights reserved. No part of this
publication may be reproduced,
stored in a retrieval system, or
transmitted in any form or by any
means, electronic, mechanical,
photocopying, recording or otherwise without the prior permission
of Moorland Publishing Co Ltd.

British Library Cataloguing in
Publication Data:
A catalogue record for this book is
available from the British Library.

Colour origination by:
P. & W. Graphics Pte Ltd, Singapore

Printed in the UK by:
Richard Clay Ltd, Bungay, Suffolk

Cover photograph: *Tombeau Bay*
(Eric Roberts)

All the illustrations have been
taken by the authors.

MPC Production Team:
Editorial: Tonya Monk
Design: Dan Clarke and John Robey
Cartography: Alastair Morrison
Typesetting: Christine Haines

Acknowledgements

The authors would like to thank
the Mauritius Government Tourist
Office in London and Mauritius;
Air Mauritius, London and the
French Government Tourist Board,
London, for all their help and
information.

Also to Madame Myreille
Blackburn for her warmth,
hospitality and guidance and
whose unfailing sense of humour
and sound advice picked us up
when we were down.

While every care has been taken to ensure that the information in this
book is as accurate as possible at the time of publication, the publisher
and authors accept no responsibility for any loss, injury or inconven-
ience sustained by anyone using this book.

CONTENTS

	Introduction	7
1	North of Port Louis	33
2	The East Coast	50
3	The South Coast	65
4	The West Coast	77
5	Port Louis	90
6	The Plateau Towns	109
7	Rodrigues	129
8	Reunion	146
	Mauritius Fact File	171
	Index	189

Key to Symbols Used in Text Margin and on Maps

Recommended walk

Nature reserve/Animal interest

Garden

Birdlife

Marine life

Other place of interest

Church/Monastery

Building of interest

Archaeological Site

Museum/Art gallery

Beautiful view/Scenery, Natural phenomenon

Cave

Watersport facilities

Key to Maps

Main road

Motorway

Boundary

City/Town

River/Lake

How To Use This Guide

This MPC Visitor's Guide has been designed to be as easy to use as possible. Each chapter covers a region or itinerary in a natural progression which gives all the background information to help you enjoy your visit. MPC's distinctive margin symbols, the important places printed in bold, and a comprehensive index enable the reader to find the most interesting places to visit with ease. At the end of each chapter an Additional Information section gives specific details such as addresses and opening times, making this guide a complete sightseeing companion. At the back of the guide the Fact File, arranged in alphabetical order, gives practical information and useful tips to help you plan your holiday — before you go and while you are there. The maps of each region show the main towns, villages, roads and places of interest, but are not designed as route maps and motorists should always use a good recommended road atlas.

INTRODUCTION

Mauritius is evocative of an island of powdery white beaches lapped by limpid pale blue lagoons, palm trees and coral reefs. It is a tropical island inhabited by a people whose warmth and hospitality cannot fail to welcome visitors who seem content to bask in the perpetual sunlight of a world which is the perfect escape for the world weary and of overwhelming interest to the inquiring traveller.

However, Mauritius is not the only refuge in this remote corner of the world. No visit, or account of a journey, to the restless and mysterious Indian Ocean would be completely satisfactory, without a glance at the two sister islands of Mauritius, geographically so close, yet so far in character and culture.

Rodrigues and Reunion are the delectable islands which, with Mauritius, form the trio known as the Mascarenes. They were named after Pedro Mascarenhas, the Portuguese Admiral, whose fleet so thankfully anchored by their uninhabited landfalls nearly five hundred years ago. Until then these remote islands had lain undisturbed since their conception millions of years before. They were formed as the direct result of a series of volcanic eruptions on the sea bed and were colonised by the seeds of sea and windborne vegetation. Attracted by the thick vegetation millions of birds made their homes in forests, mountains and even on the beaches. In Mauritius the most famous of these island birds was the ill-fated dodo. Together with a motley band of insects they lived happily beside a sea teeming with life which provided more food than they could manage.

In Mauritius volcanic activity ceased hundred of thousands of years ago. The debris left behind after its convulsions are the legacy on which the charm and beauty of its lagoons, beaches and rugged miniature mountains have been formed. The pear-shaped island occupies an area of 1,865sq km (720sq miles) and its greatest length

7

and breadth are 62 and 48km (39 and 30 miles) respectively. The central plateau, on which most of the towns are situated, was once the floor of a gigantic volcano. After it blew its top off it left behind the tatered remains of peaks which are today so characteristic of the island's scenery. Much of the debris from this Krakatoa-like explosion helped form the coastal plain and the growth of coral reefs.

High rainfall on the plateau feeds many rivers and streams providing an abundance of water. There is a great demand for irrigation in the dry coastal plains for the huge cultivation of sugar cane. Consequently the island looks fresh and green for most of the year.

The evolution of Reunion and Rodrigues proceeded very much in parallel with Mauritius. In Reunion, however, there is one striking difference. Volcanic activity has not yet abated and even now it is an island being born. It rose from the depths of the sea after Mauritius and the paroxysms of its beginnings have left deep scars in its landscape. Lying only 165km (103 miles) to the south-west of Mauritius it is the largest of the Mascarene Islands. It occupies an area of 2,512sq km (970sq miles) and consists essentially of two mountain masses. Its active volcano now only murmurs and occasionally belches molten rock to the sea around it. The coastal lowlands are narrow and often the beaches are comprised of coatings of black lava. In many places the Indian Ocean pounds weird and beautiful shapes into the rock and only on the west coast has a coral reef found a foothold. The crowning glory of Reunion are mountain ranges clothed with thick forests fed by myriads of rivers and waterfalls.

Rodrigues, a remote and forgotten island, is 653km (405 miles) east of Mauritius. Born during a separate insurgence from the sea it is the youngest and smallest of the Mascarene trio. It occupies an area of 110sq km (43sq miles) and its greatest length and breadth are 18 and 8km (11 and 5 miles) respectively. Peaks of basalt rise from a wondrous and shallow lagoon twice its size and its slopes and ravines drop smoothly to the sea. Before settlers arrived in the eighteenth century Rodrigues was a floating garden and the water surrounding it was a playground of almost every form of marine life known to man. Over the years deforestation has eroded its thin soil and islanders are constantly toiling to eke out a living in the tattered yet beautiful remnants of its glorious past.

The Mascarene Islands occupy an area in the Indian Ocean between the 19° and 22° south latitude and 55° to 64° east longitude, just inside the Tropic of Capricorn. Their nearest neighbour is the great island continent of Madagascar 805km (500 miles) to the west. They lie within the south-western Indian Ocean cyclone belt and are sometimes affected by tropical depressions.

The Mascarene Islands share a similar history and language yet each has developed independently. Most visitors head for the beaches and lagoons of Mauritius yet few consider a side trip to Reunion and even fewer venture to isolated Rodrigues. Getting to Mauritius, is not as difficult and visitors will be astounded at the delightful pot pourri of race, language, customs and culture. In Mauritius and Rodrigues the official language is English, while in Reunion it is French, yet all the islanders use Creole in all its varying forms. One thing is for certain, an insight into island life, whether in Mauritius, Rodrigues or Reunion, will reward visitors with a unique experience of this forgotten part of the Indian Ocean.

History

Before the sixteenth century European voyagers knew little of the world beyond the southern cape of Africa until explorers like Tristan da Cunha ventured forth to cross the sea now known as the Indian Ocean. Links were soon forged with the Indies and lucrative trade commenced which necessitated regular and dangerous voyages to the east. Strong winds and cyclones often forced ships hundreds of miles off course and it was those acts of nature that allowed small islands and atolls to be discovered. They were marked on early Arab charts but navigation was so primitive that the islands were often mistaken for each other. One such haven for storm-racked mariners was Mauritius and between 1507 and 1513 it was discovered by the Portuguese and named or renamed at least three times.

In 1507 Diego Fernandez Pereira, the first pilot of Tristan da Cunha, stumbled upon Mauritius during a lone voyage and after correctly identifying it as the Arabic-charted *Dinarobin* renamed it *Cerne* after the ship which he commanded. In spite of *Cerne* and her sister islands being en route to the Indies, the Portuguese were not interested in colonisation. They made no attempt at settlement but used *Cerne* as a convenient base to escape stormy weather on the long voyages between the Cape and India. The Portuguese imported pigs, monkeys and cattle so that when sailors called there would be fresh meat supplies. In addition rats and dogs escaped from their ships. The last Portuguese sailors left *Cerne* in about 1539 and it was unoccupied for over 50 years save for the occasional forays by pirates who roamed the Indian Ocean.

DUTCH SETTLEMENT 1598-1710
In 1598 the Dutch, under Admiral Van Warwyck, landed in a bay in the south-east, at what is now Grand Port, near Mahebourg. Warwyck named the bay after him and renamed the island Mauri-

tius after Prince Maurice of Nassau, the Stadtholder of Holland.

The Dutch created small settlements along the south-east coast but made no attempt to colonise the island. However they realised that the harbour in the north-west was vulnerable to invasion by the French and English who, like the Dutch, were interested in the felling of the great ebony forests. A small detachment of troops was posted at what they called Noordt Wester Haven (North West Harbour) which is the present capital, Port Louis.

By 1638 the Dutch East India Company settled. They plundered forests around the coast particularly between Flacq, Port Louis and Grand Port and sold the valuable timber at high prices in Europe. Deer was introduced to overcome food shortages and the forests were replaced with sugar cane from which they produced a potent liquor called 'arack'. In between bouts of drunkeness they imported slaves from Madagascar to work the fields and convicts from Batavia (Java) but subsequent attempts at colonisation failed because there were not enough settlers.

By 1652 many left for the Cape of Good Hope which offered better prospects than those in Mauritius. Other attempts at colonisation failed miserably through cyclones, flood, drought and plague. Food shortages, an overall inefficient administration and attacks by pirate ships compounded their desire to leave and in 1710 the last settlers abandoned Mauritius leaving a batch of runaway slaves bent on vengeance for their ill treatment.

PIRATES AND CORSAIRS IN MAURITIUS

Slaves left over from the Dutch period led a beachcomber existence, planting tobacco and a few crops. Their only visitors were crews of calling ships and ferocious pirates who by then had established their own republic in about 1685 called Libertalia in Madagascar. The republic had its own laws and language and lasted until 1730 during which time the pirates launched vicious attacks on any vessel that presented an opportunity for easy pickings. When France colonised Madagascar, many pirates drifted to Reunion and Mauritius.

With the expansion of sea trade between Europe and the Indies the pirates soon organised raiding parties on the vessels of the various East India Companies. The French, fearing for the safety of their own vessels, employed these pirates as corsairs or privateers. They were nothing more than legal pirates and continued raiding vessels claiming that they were doing it in the name of France. By the mid-eighteenth century Port Louis earned its reputation as a den of thieves where ruined adventurers, swindlers and undesirables provided the corsairs with a ready and willing outlet to dispose of their stolen goods.

Mahé de Labourdonnais, founder of Port Louis

Scorpion fish — an example of Mauritius's exotic marine wildlife

The greatest of these corsairs was Robert Surcouf (1773-1827). He came from St Malo in France and eventually retired there living from the proceeds of his privateering activities. His family is well represented in Mauritius today and searches are still being made in and around the island for his hidden treasure.

FRENCH COLONISATION 1715-1810

In 1715, the French East India Company under Captain Dufresne d'Arsel took possession of the island in the name of France; Mauritius was henceforth known as Île de France.

The first colonists landed at Warwyck Bay (Mahebourg) in 1722 where, realising the area was exposed to the winds and dangerous reefs, they moved to the comparative safety of the North West Harbour. Warwyck Bay was renamed Port Bourbon and the North West Harbour became known as Port Louis.

The transformation of Port Louis from a primitive harbour to a thriving sea port was largely due to the efforts of Bertrand Mahé de Labourdonnais, a naval officer from St Malo, in1735. As governor he introduced shipbuilding and agriculture thrived and a badly needed road system. By 1746 Port Louis was sufficiently established as a maritime base and the French East India Company supplied ships and stores for campaignes directed at the British in India.

During the Seven Years War (1756-1763) France and England continued to battle over control of the Indian Ocean and the company enlisted privateers. When the French lost the wars in India they blamed the company and accused its officials of corruption. This resulted in the offical handing over of Mauritius to the French Crown in 1767 and the affairs of the company were wound up.

During the French period slaves were imported in their thousands from Africa and Madagascar to work the sugar cane plantations. Many landed in appalling conditions at Mahebourg where they were sold to white colonists. Figures in 1767 showed that out of a population of 18,773 there were 15,023 slaves.

The French Revolution had little effect on the life of the island and if anything the influence of new ideas manifested itself in a fresh wave of loose living. The elite, bound by their common belief in slavery, had their own revolution and broke off relations with France. This state of self-autonomy lasted till 1803 when Napoleon appointed General Charles Decaen as Governor who abolished the existing government.

Decaen curried favour with the elite by allowing slavery and privateering, which were both hugely profitable, to continue. Under his governorship Port Louis became Port Napoleon and Mahebourg became Port Imperial.

BRITISH COLONISATION 1810-1968

The British East India Company was losing valuable cargoes to corsairs, so after months of blockading Port Louis, the British based themselves at Rodrigues from where they captured Bourbon (Reunion) and made several unsuccessful offensives on Île de France.

On 3 December 1810 the British, under General Abercrombie, marched into Port Napoleon where the French surrendered. Île de France, Port Napoleon and Port Imperial reverted to their former names, Mauritius, Port Louis and Mahebourg.

For an island that had caused the British so much trouble in the past General Abercrombie was remarkably generous towards the inhabitants. The French colonists were allowed to keep their land and slaves, those wishing to leave the island were offered a free passage back to France and civilians were permitted to retain their customs, culture and language and compensated for damage to property.

By eliminating Mauritius as a privateers base and establishing a garrison and a governor, Britain had achieved maritime supremacy in the Indian Ocean and voyages between the Cape and India could be undertaken in comparative safety. English became the official language and the island retained its French character.

Robert Farquhar, the first English governor, announced that civil and judicial administration would be unchanged. Those who refused to take an oath of allegiance to the British Crown were asked to leave Mauritius within a reasonable time. Under his governorship sugar production increased, Port Louis was transformed into a free port, roads were built and trade flourished.

Sugar production developed into a major foreign income earner and the planters relied increasingly on slave labour in spite of the 1807 Act abolishing it in the British Empire. Judge John Jeremie was appointed Attorney-General in Mauritius and arrived from England in 1832 to announce abolition without indemnity to a hostile reception of sugar planters and slave owners.

Slavery was finally abolished in 1835 but not before the owners received £2,000,000 compensation. Shortly afterwards thousands of Indians from the backstreets of Madras, Calcutta and Bombay were encouraged to emigrate to Mauritius with promises of a labour contract that included a salary and accommodation and a passage home. They arrived, like the African slaves before them, in dreadful conditions at Port Louis where they were housed in temporary depots and distributed to the sugar estates. They were paid a pittance, subjected to harsh treatment and forced to work long hours. In short, these indentured labourers or 'coolies', were slaves by another name and were to form the majority of the population.

The 'coolie trade' reached such unprecedented heights in the mid-nineteenth century that it had to be regulated with the establishment of an Immigration Department. Things improved only slightly and in 1872 a Royal Commission was appointed to look into the problems of Indian immigration. Their living standards became more tolerable and when immigration ceased in 1909 and another Royal Commission made recommendations for social and political reform many Indians had settled permanently in Mauritius and indeed formed the majority of the population.

In 1907 an Indian lawyer called Manilal Doctor was sent by the young Mohandas Gandhi to shake the Indian community from their apathy and arouse political interest. Only 2 per cent of the population were entitled to vote and the Indians were totally unrepresented.

In 1936 the Labour Party was formed and persuaded the Indians to take political action and campaign for better working conditions. A series of strikes throughout 1937 and again in 1943 brought the sugar industry to a standstill until the British responded by drawing up a plan for constitutional reform.

The real turning point in modern history came when the first elections under universal adult suffrage were held in March 1959. These were won by the Labour Party under a Hindu doctor, Seewoosagur Ramgoolam (later Sir) who later was the first Prime Minister.

SINCE INDEPENDENCE

Mauritius achieved independance on 12 March 1968 with Ramgoolam as the Prime Minister who formed a coalition government. Mauritius has the distinction of being one of the most stable countries in the developing world.

Mauritius is a sovereign democratic state within the Commonwealth. It includes Rodrigues, with which it is politically integrated, and several island dependencies, the main ones being Agalega and St Brandon in the Cargados Carajos group. The islands are administered by the Outer Islands Development Corporation in Port Louis and permission, which is difficult to obtain, must be sought in writing from them stating the purpose of the visit.

Agalega lies 933km (578 miles) to the north of Mauritius and consists of two islands, north and south, covering a total of 26sq km (10sq miles). The inhabitants, mainly workers from Mauritius, fish and grow coconuts.

St Brandon is 447km (277 miles) to the north-east and is nothing more than a group of sand banks, shoals and islets. Most of its inhabitants are fishermen working on 6 month government contracts. Thousands of sea birds frequent St Brandon and guano along

The thumb-shaped Pouce Mountain with sugar cane fields in foreground

Edible coeur de palmiste *or heart of palm is germinated in seedling bags*

16 • Visitor's Guide: Mauritius, Rodrigues & Reunion

with fishing are the main industries.

Mauritius claims sovereignty over the island of Tromelin, 560km (347 miles) to the north-east, in spite of it having been occupied by the French since before the capitualtion terms of 1810. The French rear turtles in its waters for transportation to Reunion.

Mention should also be made of Diego Garcia in the Chagos Archipelago, 1,931km (1,200 miles) to the north-east, which used to belong to Mauritius but now forms part of the British Indian Ocean Territory. Today Diego Garcia is the principal American base in the Indian Ocean and is closed to visitors.

For administrative purposes, Mauritius is divided into nine districts with the island of Rodrigues forming the tenth. Executive power is vested in Her Majesty Queen Elizabeth II whose official representative is the Governor-General. The government is based on a Westminster style democracy while still retaining its traditional links with Africa, India and Europe.

Since independence Mauritius has changed drastically from a sugar producing island to a newly industrialised nation. For many, Mauritius was synonymous with the dodo or the rare penny orange and twopenny blue stamps, while others confused the island with Mauritania or Martinique. It lay somewhere in the backwaters of an ocean but nobody really knew where.

Today the country is back on the map and much of its economic success is attributable to a policy of diversification from its traditional one crop industry, sugar, to tourism and textiles.

Mauritius has become self-sufficient in agriculture through land rotation farming techniques and interline cropping. Potatoes, tomatoes, onions and garlic, maize, groundnuts and poultry are some of the products widely available to the domestic market. In addition the farming community is active in the production of milk, cattle, pigs, sheep, goat and deer. However cattle breeding is expensive compared to the cost of importing meat.

Just under half of the land is given over to agriculture with sugar accounting for not less than 93 per cent. Sugar is Mauritius oldest industry and remains one of the most important agricultural activities. However the diversification policy has resulted in a manpower shortage and the industry is having to invest heavily in labour saving modern equipment. Visits to sugar factories are possible by prior arrangement with the management or through a tour operator. The sugar cane fields are at their most beautiful in the months just prior to harvesting in June when undulating hillsides and flatlands are clothed in a patchwork of purple plumage signifying varying degrees of ripeness.

In 1971 the government, aware of the difficulties of relying on a one crop economy, created the Export Processing Zone (EPZ) as a means of diversification into manufacturing and textiles. The number of enterprises operating in Mauritius rose from ten since its inception in 1971 to over five hundred in 1990 and the EPZ now competes with sugar and tourism in the nation's economy. Clothing and knitwear made in Mauritius can be found in stores throughout Europe, America and the Far East. Other successful activities within the EPZ include diamond cutting, the assembly of watches, production of watch parts, electronic components, ships models and leather garments. More recently anthuriums, beautiful wax-like flowers that last up to 6 weeks, are being commercially cultivated for large scale export to Europe.

Mauritius has made great inroads into tourism since it first opened its doors to a group of travellers in the 1950s Promoted in holiday brochures as one of those faraway places associated with the dodo and desert island dreams, it is a country of diverse cultures justifying the tourist office's claim to being 'the most cosmopolitan island in the sun' with a smiling, natural and charming people. Blessed with an almost perfect year round climate and hotels with excellent service, comfortable accommodation and a full range of water and land sports, the visitor is transported to another world of dazzling white beaches, deep blue lagoons and an enchanting mountain scenery.

Food, Drink and Entertainment

The mixture of the island's various races is reflected in Mauritian cuisine. Hence, spicy curries, concoctions of tropical fruit and vegetables, and Chinese and European food lure the visitor to the many restaurants in Port Louis and on the popular west and north-west coasts. Throughout the year hotels provide Creole nights with *sega* dancing and theme barbecues. The food, while beautifully presented, is considerably toned down to cater for the palate of an international clientele. However, traditional delicacies like *coeur de palmiste* or 'millionaires salad', made from the heart of a 7-year-old palm is a light, refreshing salad and can be eaten with smoked marlin, another of the island's specialities. Venison curry is another favourite, a rich meaty dish eaten with boiled rice.

Seafoods is expensive in the hotel restaurants. For local foods, try the snacks available at street stalls. *Gateaux piments*, a dough of green chillies and split peas fried to a golden brown and *dholl puree*, thin pancakes cooked on a griddle are spicy and are freshly prepared.

Fresh pineapples and bananas and imported apples are available year round. Mango, lychees and passion fruit can be found from December to February. The market in Port Louis should not be missed for its picturesque domes of exotic fruit and vegetables.

All imported wines and spirits are subject to heavy taxes but the local wine made from imported grape must and local beers and spirits make an acceptable alternative. White rum, made from sugar molasses is bottled under the Green Island label but others like Mainstay Dry Cane Spirit and Old Mill Rum and the local whiskies are almost as good and half the price.

Much of the night life centres round the hotels which provide music and dancing, theme evenings and in some cases casinos. Away from the hotels, the Amicale Casino at Port Louis provides Chinese games only while the casino at Curepipe has roulette and blackjack. There are lively discoteques and piano bars situated in the plateau towns and cinemas in Port Louis, Rose Hill and Quatre Bornes. There are only two theatres: one in Port Louis that is rarely open for production and the Plaza at Rose Hill.

Mauritius has excellent facilities for water sports and specialises in big game fishing in the deep waters beyond the reef. With its mountainous interior, walking enthusiasts can enjoy climbing and walking either independently or with an organised group. From May to November, horse racing is in full swing with weekly Saturday meetings held at the Champs de Mars Race Course in Port Louis. Athletic and sporting events are advertised in the local press.

Flora and Fauna

Mauritius was once covered in thick evergreen mountain forest. The waters teemed with armies of giant turtles, dugongs and fish. Bats, birds and insects feasted on natural resources and the dodo waddled along deserted beaches blissfully unaware than when man arrived in the sixteenth century he would shake the harmony of its existence. In doing so, for want of survival or commercial gain, he upset forever the delicate ecological balance that had existed for so many years.

Many of these creatures shared the same fate as the dodo. The gigantic turkey-like bird, with a hard twisted beak and tiny wings had never experienced danger. It had forgotten how to fly and made easy prey for the first Dutch settlers. Within a few years it was wiped off the face of the earth.

The demise of the dodo was followed by the decimation of virgin forest. Shipbuilding, sugar a road and rail network for its transportation, the creation of upland settlements and the introduction of animals and invasive plants over three centuries of human

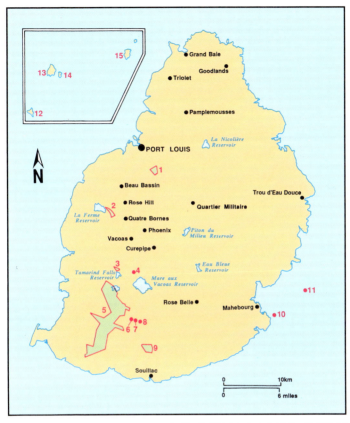

Key to Nature Reserves				
1	Pouce	6	Les Mares	11	Îlot Mariannes
2	Corps de Garde	7	Gouly Père	12	Coin de Mire
3	Cabinet	8	Boise Sec	13	Île Plate
4	Perrier	9	Combo	14	Îlot Gabriel
5	Macchabée-Bel Ombre	10	Île aux Aigrettes	15	Île Ronde

settlement destroyed the island's indigenous forests.

The need to preserve the indigenous forests of Mauritius, as in other countries of the world, was realised too late and today less than 1 per cent of the original forest remains. Most of it lies to the south of Plaine Champagne in the Bel Ombre-Macchabee Forest. Great efforts are being made by the government and the Forestry Department to preserve what is left by educating the public to appreciate their ecological value. In this context patches of forest in other parts of the island have been declared nature reserves. Some of them are only a few square kilometres and are fenced off so as to encourage regeneration of indigenous trees and plants.

Today the forests are classified into three areas essentially consisting of Crown Forest Lands, the 'Pas Geometrique' and privately owned forest lands. The Crown Forest Lands contain the nature reserves along with areas given over to tea plantations. The State-owned 'Pas Geometrique' forms a narrow coastal belt, which is occupied by public beaches, although much of it is leased to the hotel industry or used for grazing and tree planting programmes. Finally the privately owned forest lands are found in the upper slopes of mountains where many areas are densely covered with native forest or thickets of Travellers Palm.

Strict laws govern the use of forests including unauthorised felling or removal of trees, illegal possession of wood and trespassing on Crown Forest lands. In spite this, forest recreation is becoming more popular with tourists and locals, and nature trails have been marked out in the Macchabee Forest. Walking independently is possible but a permit must be obtained from the Conservator of Forests. It may be advisable and preferable to join an organised walk with a tour operator or a local walking group, such as Centre d'Excursion de Beau Bassin, when permission has been obtained. Always obtain the permission of the owner if entering private forest.

There are fifteen nature reserves. Six are offshore islands and nine are on the mainland. The smallest of these, Perrier, Cabinet, Les Mares, Gouly Pere and Bois Sec, are dotted around the Tamarin Falls and Grand Bassin area and contain tiny traces of indigenous forest. Slightly larger nature reserves are found on the slopes of Le Pouce and Corps de Garde Mountains and at Combo in the Savanne Mountains. The largest is Macchabee-Bel Ombre which sweeps southwards from Mare Longue Reservoir across Plaine Champagne along the south-west slopes of the Savanne Mountains. It and Round Island are scientific reserves and are recognised under Category 1 of the United Nations List of National Parks and Protected Areas.

But for all man's destruction the island is green and verdant. Sugar cane clothes the landscape and deep green velvety clusters of tea plantations stretch around the highlands of Curepipe. The island is a riot of colour throughout the year with bougainvillea, hibiscus, orchid, poinsietta and oleander growing in towns, parks, gardens and coastal areas. In summer flamboyant and frangipani trees burst into brilliant bloom along the roadsides.

Indigenous trees such as the ebony are protected species, and are found in the uplands of the Macchabee Forest along with the natte tree and tambalacoque or dodo tree. The seed of the tambalacoque was so hard that it was difficult to germinate. Legend has it that the dodo is supposed to have softened the seed by passing it through its digestive system thereby enabling it to germinate more easily. A specimen of the Bois Colophane batard a sister of the extremely rare colophane can be seen at the Pamplemousses Botanical Gardens. The resin from these trees was used in the manufacture of plasters, ointments and varnishes.

Imported trees such as pine and eucalyptus grow profusely in the plateau areas. Great matted forests of Chinese Guava can be seen in Plaine Champagne and the Black River Gorges with fan shaped Travellers Palm while bottle palms, looking like Chianti bottles, adorn roundabouts between Port Louis and Curepipe.

It would be hard to do justice to a Mauritian beach without reference to the whispering filao or casuarina trees. They are a feature of virtually every beach and their feathery dark green branchlets provide an excellent shelter from winds and tropical sun. The tree was introduced to Mauritius by the French explorer and cartographer Abbe Alexis Rochon in 1778. Nearly one hundred years later the British Governor, Sir Arthur Gordon, ordered that the casuarina, being salt-tolerant, quick growing and undemanding, should be planted around the coastline as part of a tree and water conservation system.

In the lowland areas imported trees consist of acacia, coconut palm, albizia, the badamier or Indian Almond and the banyan. The mangrove is found in the brackish swamps of the east coast.

Public gardens are found all over the island and are worth visiting. Fine specimens of trees and plants can be found at Pamplemousses Botanical Gardens 7 miles (4km) to the north of Port Louis. Curepipe boasts its own small, but beautiful, botanical garden where, the viah palm from Madagascar grows in an attractive lake.

The only indigenous mammals of Mauritius were two species of fruit bat, one of which is now extinct and three species of insectivorous bats. A cousin, the Rodrigues fruit bat was until recently also threatened with extinction. A successful colony now exists at the Government Aviaries at Black River.

The Mauritius Golden Bat or flying fox is more common. It swoops over highland forests at nightfall in search of fruit. Its flesh, sweetened by its diet, according to some Mauritians, makes a tasty curry.

The deer was introduced from Java in 1639 to supply meat to the first settlers. Deer farming is well established in the Case Noyale and Le Morne areas. Less timid deer can be seen in the enclosure at Pamplemousses Gardens.

Other imported species are the Macaque monkey which was introduced by the Portuguese in 1528 from Malaysia. They move in great bands in the forests of the Black River area and can be trained as domestic pets. The tenrec, a tailess hedgehog-like creature came from Madagascar in the late nineteenth century and thrives in gardens and cane fields living on insects. The mongoose from India, was introduced in 1900 to combat the rat population that threatened the sugar cane. It multiplied so fast that it has in fact become a nuisance. Wild boar are the descendants of the domestic pig introduced by the Portuguese. They feed on sugar cane and their flesh is very sweet. Other introduced animals include the Indian hare, goats, dogs and the hump-backed cow or zebu from Madagascar.

Mention must be made of life's annoyances. They are best described in the words of Nicholas Pike, the American Consul, who arrived in Mautitius in 1867 and made the mistake of staying the night in a dubious downtown Port Louis hotel where he observed: 'What with bugs, mosquitoes, and cockroaches (to say nothing of centipedes six inches long!), the knocking about of billiard balls till late, and the loud laughter and gossiping of coloured servants, sleep was impossible. The mosquito curtains were not properly beaten, and whole families lay in wait for their unsuspecting victim; the cockroaches ate my clothes; the ants got into my trunks; lizards crept over the walls, and rats, bold as lions, were all over the house'.

Pike's pests are not as prolific today. Nature and progress have worked together to confine them to their proper place and visitors need not feel apprehensive about staying at the modern luxury hotels or eating in any one of the fine restaurants. In Mauritius such animals are regarded as an occasional tropical nuisance.

Besides three species of house geckos there are several tree lizards. *Phelsuma ornata* is found on palm trees and the male is identifiable by its luminous green, black and white striped neck and its red spotted back; *Phelsuma cepediana* scurries up the banana and traveller's palm and has a spotted green and red back: *Phelsuma guimbeaui* is found on older trees and is entirely green with red spots and a blue tipped tail. The agama, commonly and wrongly referred to as the chameleon by Mauritians, comes from India and is brown or green with black markings. It has a slight crest on the head, long legs and a long tail.

There are no poisonous snakes on the island. The only snake is the couleuvre from India which is pale brown with chocolate and gold markings on its back. It is nocturnal and aggressive if disturbed.

Bottle palms at Le Val Nature Park

Most of the birds found in Mauritius have been introduced. Out of an estimated twenty-six endemic birds only nine species remain. Of these only one, the pic-pic or grey white eye a small greyish bird with a white rump is common. Vulnerable species include the cuckoo shrike, the merle and the olive white-eye. The population of the Mascarene paradise-flycatcher is small and its survival in the wild is threatened by nest-raiding monkeys while the delightful scarlet red headed Mauritius fody or Cardinal, reputed to bring luck if it enters the home, is in danger of disappearing.

Funded by international conservation agencies captive breeding of the Mauritius Kestrel has been a great success although the population is still fragile. Even greater success was achieved with the Pink Pigeon another endangered species,which can be seen at Casela Bird Park. The most endangered endemic bird in Mauritius is the Echo Parakeet of which perhaps about a dozen remain. Experiments to breed it in captivity are being carried out at the Black River government aviary to save it from total extinction.

Introduced or exotic birds thrive well in Mauritius. They can be observed pecking in the sand by beachside bungalows, in open country, at Pamplemousses Gardens or in the aviaries at Casela Bird Park. Birds from India include the red whiskered bulbul, identifiable by its black witch-like crest and red feathered bill, the bluish-black House Crow and the Mynah, a large brownish bird with a yellow bill and yellow feet which can be taught to speak. The spotted dove and the zebra dove from Malaysia can be seen feeding on open land. The ring necked parakeet, not to be confused with the Echo parakeet (a brilliant large green bird that was introduced in 1886) can be seen where there is a surplus of grain.

Serpent Island (which has no snakes) is the habitat of colonies of seabirds, including the blue faced booby the noddy and the sooty tern. Colonies of the wedge-tailed shearwater, the Trinidade petrel and the graceful red-tailed tropic bird nest on Round Island. Its white-tailed cousin swoops through the gorges of the Black River. Also known as the *paille-en-queue* (straw in the tail) it has been adapted as the Air Mauritius logo.

Shore and marsh birds, driven to Mauritius by air currents or bad weather, include the whimbrel, the common and curlew sandpiper, the sand plover the grey plover and the turnstone.

Mountains

There are three main mountain ranges in Mauritius. The Moka Range around Port Louis covers a distance of approximately 20km (12 miles) beginning at Mount Ory and finishing at Nouvelle

Decouverte. The Black River chain stretches from Rempart Mountain to the south of Bambous village as far as Le Morne in the southwest and continues to form the Savanne Mountains in the extreme south. Finally the Grand Port range at 24km (15 miles) starts at Mount Lagrave and stretches to the mouth of the Grand River South East. Delightful, diminutive and picturesque, the mountains seem to pop up from the landscape in the least expected places providing a natural compass for anyone who thought there was no way out of the miles and miles of sugar cane fields.

Adventurous walks and climbs can be made of the mountain ranges but paths are not waymarked, the ascents can be dangerous and some of the land is privately owned. Tour operators can organise individual or group walks on request and sometimes excursions can be made with local walking groups. Two publications of interest to the intrepid walker and mountaineer are *Mountains of Mauritius* by Robert V.R. Marsh and Climbing and *Mountain Walking in Mauritius* by Alexander Ward. The former is available in bookshops in Mauritius but the latter is sadly out of print. However a copy is available for reference at the Mauritius Institute library in Port Louis.

Marine Life

The island is almost completely encircled by one of the world's finest coral reefs. Through millions of years this beautiful cluster of calciferous polyps has built upon a precarious foothold on the shallow sea bed near shore to form a veritable underwater world — a vast world in which thousands of marine species live, eat, work and die allowing the whole universe to proliferate. A coral reef can only exist in salt water so at river estuaries and at the sea's surface it perishes. As the great ocean waves break upon its extremities a translucent white pencil-thin white line divides the deep blue of the Indian Ocean from the irridescent green of the lagoon. It is this phenomenon occuring at distances varying from nothing to a few kilometres from the shore which is the unfailing characteristic of a real tropical island.

Brightly coloured fish weave through coral gardens, great moray eels lurk in caves, and crustaceans scavenge the reef amidst a riot of ornamental underwater vegetation. Organised diving trips to selected sites can be arranged through hotel diving schools who provide equipment. The snorkeller can easily sample some of the ocean delights and need not stray far to gaze casually upon the amusing antics of delightful trumpet, clown and box fish to name but a few of the hundreds of reef residents.The less adventurous can experience lagoon life by taking a trip in a glass bottom boat.

Some creatures command respect. Divers should be wary of the great moray eel and the lionfish with its delicate feathery fins and the stonefish or laff with its venomous dorsal spine. Both can inflict serious wounds which, if left untreated, can be fatal. Species of interest to big game fishermen, such as shark, barracuda, marlin, sailfish, tuna and wahoo confine themselves to areas beyond the reef.

In spite of the abundance of marine life the reef has been over-exploited in recent years. Studies show that there has been a dramatic decline in population attributable to pollution from domestic and touristic outlets, coral attacks by the Crown of Thorns starfish and illegal dynamiting of the reef by fishermen. The Mauritius Marine Conservation Group is an organisation set up to highlight public awareness of damage to the coral reef by educating schoolchildren and the public by slide shows and lectures. Their work includes the creation of artificial reefs by sinking barges in areas where the reef has been destroyed thus providing a fresh habitat for marine life.

Shell collecting has also resulted in a population decline and the sale of shells from Mauritian beaches has been banned. Exportation by tourists is limited to three. Shells found in shops or those offered for sale by beach vendors are likely to have been imported from the Phillipines. The best time to collect shells is immediately after a cyclone. However, certain species of the cone and cowrie shells emit poisonous injections if trodden upon or handled carelessly.

People and Culture

Europeans are struck with confusion on attempting to pronounce the name of Mauritius' airport. Even Mauritians, who for years have called it Plaisance, have difficulty in rolling their tongues around 'Sir Seewoosagur Ramgoolam International Airport' and prefer to abbreviate it to SSR. But this is a name visitors will frequently encounter. He was the country's first Prime Minister and following his death in 1985, a street, hospital, botanical gardens, a tug, public beach and an airport have been named after him. He is to Mauritians what Attaturk is to the Turks or Churchill is to the British.

Confusion lingers when the visitor leaves the plane and steps into the arrivals hall of SSR Airport. He is greeted by a mural of the Great Wall of China and a flurry of brown-skinned airport officials, all speaking perfect English with a French twang. Outside in the main concourse Chinese, European and Indian bank clerks change foreign currency into rupees completing the transaction with such conversational ease and fluency that foreign visitors wonder if they haven't been accidentally re-routed to any one of the great continents.

Trois Mamelles (Three Breasts) with Rempart Mountain to the right, as seen from Curepipe

Mauritians are such a diverse people

The confusion subsides when the visitor realises that Mauritius was uninhabited until the seventeenth century. There are no indigenous people and today the population is composed of Indians, Africans, Europeans and Chinese who are so culturally integrated that when asked 'What nationality are you?' simply reply 'Mauritian'. The island's colonial history under French and British rule and influence from India, Africa and China have produced a unique racial harmony with each ethnic group adhering to its cultural and religious beliefs yet still maintaining a Mauritian unity.

The population comprises three main groups: Indo-Mauritians, Creoles or people of mixed European and African origin (sometimes called the 'general population') and Sino-Mauritians. Although many Indian and Chinese languages are spoken, the lingua franca is Creole, a pidgin French. When slaves were imported from different parts of Africa and Madagascar they brought their individual languages and culture with them. To overcome the language problem in a new country they adopted Creole which was easy to learn and had no grammatical rules. As far back as 1729, Creole was used as the common language between slaves of various ethnic origins and their French masters. English, however, is the official language.

Indo-Mauritians today are mainly the descendants of sugar workers who came as indentured labourers from India. Others came from the merchant classes and held the monopoly of the trade in drapery and food grains. Indo-Mauritians are sub-divided into further groups: Hindus, Tamils and Moslems.

The Hindus came from northern India and form the largest ethnic group. Throughout the island, in small towns and villages, their houses are festooned with red and white flags and the gardens often contain a small shrine erected to their god. The Tamils originate from southern India and are renowned for their awe inspiring rituals and practices, such as fire and sword walking. The smallest group of Indo-Mauritians are the Muslims who came from the Gujerati speaking region of west India and Bombay.

The second group are the Creoles or 'general population'. Creole originally meant anyone from European descent born outside France but in Mauritius it has come to include anyone who was born in Mauritius but excluding the Indians and Chinese. Creoles are the descendants of African or Malagasy slaves who arrived in great numbers under French and British rule.

The 'general population' includes a small group of Franco-Mauritians who are the white descendants of the original French colonists. They still speak the pure French of their ancestors and retain a sophisticated lifestyle. Many are involved in management or finance and control much of the sugar and tourism industry.

The smallest ethnic group are the Chinese or Sino-Mauritians whose forefathers arrived as sailors, artisans and small traders at the invitation of the British government in 1826. By the 1920s they had gained control of the retail trade in the Chinese Quarter in Port Louis and established their own chamber of commerce. They are renowned for their business acumen and hold key jobs in accountancy and banking. Many run their own retailing businesses from the small corner shop to large companies.

The government has been careful to encourage racial and religious harmony and while at one time intermarriage was frowned upon it is becoming more frequent and acceptable.

There are eighty-seven religious denominations but the main religions practised are Hinduism, Christianity and Islam. Christianity was the first to take root and today about a quarter of a million inhabitants are Roman Catholics. Hinduism, in its varying forms, is practised by just over half of the population with about 16 per cent devoted to Islam. Since the majority of the Sino-Mauritians are Roman Catholics. Buddhism is diminishing although Chinese festivals are still celebrated. Many religious festivals are public holidays and give an indication of the delicate balancing trick of preserving each culture without allowing one to swamp the other.

Festivals, often designated public holidays, reflect the religious diversity of the island. These include the Festival of Pere Laval, celebrated by Roman Catholics on the night of the 7 and 8 September, the awe-inspiring Cavadee celebrated by the Tamil speaking Hindus during January and the Maha Shivaratree, celebrated by the Hindi speaking Hindus in February.

The Sino-Mauritians celebrate the Chinese Spring Festival, eight days before the Chinese New Year with a thorough spring cleaning of their homes. They decorate the interiors with red streamers inscribed with wishes of peace and prosperity. New Year's Day is a holiday for the Chinese community.

Divali or Festival of Light is celebrated by Hindus during a new moon night between October and November. It marks the triumph of good over evil and the prevalence of knowledge over ignorance. It is a happy gay occasion when earthenware lamps are illuminated throughout the island while children detonate firecrackers amidst music and dancing.

Ganga Asnan is a time of purification when Hindus converge into the sea and offer gifts to the goddess Ganga. The River Ganges flows into the Indian Ocean and the waters surrounding Mauritius are considered sacred. All public beaches are very crowded during this time and lifeguard patrols are on duty in case of accidents.

Eid-Ul-Fitr is an important Moslem event. It marks the end of the long fast kept during the Islamic observance of Ramadam when the faithful do not eat between sunrise and sunset. Ul-Fitr, literally translated, means 'break fast' and is of major spiritual importance.

Independence Day is celebrated on 12 March at the Champs de Mars Race Course in Port Louis. It is a grand occasion, full of pomp and ceremony, attended by the Prime Minister and the Governor General, the Legislative Assembly and diplomatic representatives. It is a unique opportunity to witness the national unity of Mauritians when ethnic groups give displays of music, song and dance.

Historical links with France and Britain can be seen in the nation's architecture but many of the grand colonial houses that used to grace the land have disappeared or fallen into a state of disrepair.

In the centre of Port Louis, modern concrete and glass office buildings soar skyward from the remains of a patchwork of dilapidated Creole houses. Large colonial houses can be found in the country areas. They are privately owned or managed and are sometimes used as venues for meetings with royalty or heads of states. Some are open to the public and afford an insight into life under French and British colonialism with beautiful antique furniture, polished wooden floors and high ceilinged rooms.

There are many statues, obelisks, tombs and historic buildings throughout the island which have been declared 'National Monuments'. In Port Louis alone there are sixty-six and a National Monuments Board was created in 1985 to encourage Mauritians to become aware of the need to preserve their heritage. In the streets leading to Marie Reine de la Paix in Port Louis, examples of delightfully restored wooden Creole houses can be seen, some with small courtyards of potted flowers, tropical fruit trees and giant rubber plants.

A typical Creole house is constructed of wood with a decorative carved wooden valence on the eaves around the roof and windows. The verandah is spacious and long open windows ensure that air circulates inside the house. All windows are built with wooded shutters that can be closed during a cyclone.

Cyclones have caused sometimes severe damage to buildings, particularly to those built from wood. In 1962, Cyclone Carol, the most violent in human memory with gusts of up to 306kph (190mph), left thousands homeless and the sugar crop was reduced by half. The cyclone brought about a major shift in building habits

Mauritian fruit seller

with the result that all buildings are now concrete structures with concrete flat roofs. In spite of their unimaginative design they are safe and private dwellings are made more attractive by swathing them in tropical flowers and vegetation. However in the area around Blue Baie, new cyclone proof housing complexes have been constructed in the traditional Creole style.

Local handicrafts production has suffered in recent years and government efforts are being made to rekindle enthusiasm by providing workshop training and funding. Patchwork Creole dolls, tablemats and embroidery can be bought at SPES and at women's Self Help Boutique in Quatre Bornes. Other items are displayed at the National Handicraft Centre in Port Louis and all markets sell traditional *tentes* or baskets. The model sailing ship industry is well established and most companies can arrange for models to be packaged and transported seperately. Work of local handicraft companies is sometimes shown in hotel foyers.

Mauritians have their own brand of music and dancing in the *sega* which it is believed to have come from Africa. It is a wild, sensual dance inherited from the slaves who expressed their feelings of sadness, fears, hopes and expectations in the form of song and movement. It is traditionally performed by pairs of the opposite sex although commercialised versions in hotels consist of a troupe of beautiful, dusky women who gyrate their hips in unison to the accompaniment of electric guitars and drums in colourful, lively and well produced cabarets that might well distract the visitor from the original meaning of the dance.

The original musical instruments accompanying the *sega* are the *ravanne*, a tambourine made from goat's skin, the *tantam*, a kind of bow to which a gourd is attached and plucked in time to the drum beat, the *maravanne*, a wooden box half filled with dried beans or stones which is shaken like a maracas, and a steel triangle.

The lyrics are always sung in Creole, normally about the plight of slaves. However, modern songs are full of humour and colourful expression and more suggestive than the former laments. Modern *sega* cassettes and records are widely available.

Cultural activity has been promoted by the setting up of a number of cultural centres in collaboration with friendly countries. These include the British Council at Rose Hill, the Mahatma Gandhi Institute at Moka and the African Cultural Centre, the China Cultural Centre and the French Cultural Centre at Bell Village. There are several Mauritian organisations which meet regularly in Great Britain and two newspapers who have offices in London. For details see the Fact File.

1
NORTH OF PORT LOUIS

M any visitors to Mauritius head for the well established north-
west coast. A good motorway links Port Louis with Pamplemousses and Mapou with easy access along well surfaced roads to
the main resorts of Trou aux Biches, Grand Baie and Pereybere.

The coast from Trou aux Biches to Grand Baie is one of the loveliest
of the island displaying an unbroken chain of powder white beaches
and gentle crystal lagoons. Hotels, guest houses and private bungalows are plentiful and a generally good infrastructure of roads
enable the visitor to experience the sights and sounds of Port Louis
only half an hour's drive away and the well trodden tourist trails of
the coast. That is not to say that the north is over developed. Tourism
has been carefully monitored to preserve the natural environment
and it would be impossible to find a crowded beach anywhere along
this coast.

The north of the island comprises the administrative districts of
Pamplemousses and Rivière du Rempart and is composed of
flatlands where villages and towns are surrounded by sugar cane
and tobacco fields.

Trou aux Biches, is undoubtedly one of the most popular resorts
attracting an international clientele. A former fishing village it is now
given over to tourism with the Trou aux Biches Village Hotel
dominating some 2km (1 mile) of the best part of the beach. The hotel
attracts younger groups, families and couples and offers water and
land based sporting activities such as waterskiing, windsurfing,
snorkelling, sailing, glass bottom boat, floodlit tennis courts and a 9
hole golf course free to all guests. An extra charge is made for scuba,
deep sea fishing and trimaran cruises. Non-guests, for a small
entrance fee, may take part in a nightly entertainments programme
which include *sega* dance shows and a casino. Boat excursions to

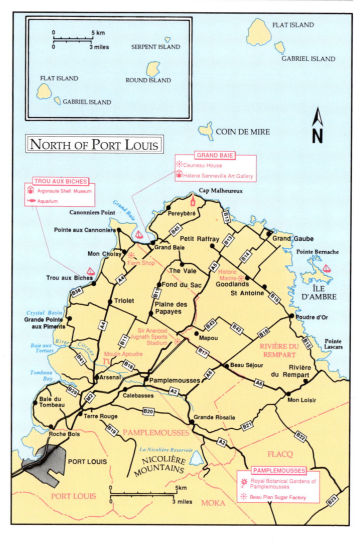

Pointe aux Piments and Baie aux Tortues and sunset cruises for the romantic feature along with helicopter tours for the adventurous. The hotel offers honeymoon packages with fruit, flowers and wine and can arrange weddings for foreigners.

Although the hotel entrance is controlled by guard no beach in

Mauritius is private and it is possible to walk along the beach to the hotel from the old village one kilometre south of the hotel. The Police Station is located midway between Trou aux Biches Hotel and the village on the coast road where the B38 forms a junction with the B36 road to Triolet. There is a coin box inside the Police Station for public use. A mobile food wagon opposite sells snacks and drinks and the Souvenir Snack restaurant serves delicious portions of chow mein and rice based dishes.

Along the main B38 coast road bungalows are available for private renting. Enquiries can be made at Chez Popo, Chinese grocer shop where everything from postcards to pork chops and car/bicycle hire is supplied to both tourists and locals. There is a postcard/souvenir shop next door and a post box but it is advisable to post mail either at the hotel or at a post office as collections can be erratic.

Sega *dancing is a popular entertainment on Mauritius*

In Trou aux Biches village, just across the road from the Lagon Bleu Restaurant a taxi stand and bus stop provide services along the coast to Grand Baie. The comfortable restaurant overlooks the sea and serves mainly Creole and European fare and seafood. Below there is a bar mainly patronised by the local fishermen and another small Chinese grocer's store. The Etoile de mer Hotel almost next door, has an open-air bar/restaurant and is a good stop for a quiet, unrushed drink. A pleasant hour may be spent watching locals barter for freshly caught fish at the fish landing station on the beach. Here the beach is rocky. If planning to explore between the rocks it is advisable to wear boots or water shoes for protection against sea urchins and the occasional laff.

A few metres away the Trou aux Biches Aquarium offers a fascinating glimpse of the teeming marine life around Mauritius and is the next best experience for those visitors who are unable or unwilling to witness the exciting underwater for real.

One million litres of water are pumped daily into the 36 tanks on an open circuit and sterilized by ozone and ultra violet rays. One tank 16m (52ft) long contains 150,000 litres of water where sharks, moray eels, murines and other deep water specimens are kept. Lagoon fish including the graceful sea turtles are kept in a smaller tank 7m (23ft) long containing 35,000 litres of water. Exhibits of reef fauna are contained in the remaining tanks. There are some 250 species including the laff or stone fish.

The laff is one of the ocean's nastiest residents. It is an ugly creature camouflaged to resemble a lump of gnarled rock. Closer inspection reveals that it has an inverted 'V' shaped chin giving it the impression that it is permanently recovering from the effects of a severe upper cut. It embeds itself among rocks in muddy waters leaving its eyes barely visible. Tread on him and you will know it. The dorsal spines inject a venomous sting which if untreated within 6 hours can be fatal. Fishermen rely on nature's remedies by applying a poultice of herbs but for the uninitiated immediate transfer to a hospital is essential.

In addition there is a pleasantly laid out shop selling beachwear, postcards, film, jewellery, imported shells and mainly French language books and magazines. An excellent illustrated book called *Fish of Mauritius* is available in English and French, by the founder of the aquarium, Alain Cornic, is also on sale.

Roughly corrugated shacks, the homes of friendly fishing families line the coastal road. On the left is the Argonaute Shell Museum which is really a shop displaying unusual gifts and souvenirs. A school nearby doubles as a cyclone refuge centre. The road turns slightly inland and the rocky coast is hidden by filaos trees and bungalows. To the left fields of sugar cane sweep to the foothills of the Moka range. The Hotel de la Sirene is a pleasant five roomed pension with bar/restaurant on a patio. Almost opposite is La Laguna Restaurant with tables set on verandahs overlooking the ocean.

Just beyond Villas Pointe aux Biches there is a forest of filaos trees. Walk up the raised bank to get to the beach which is a mixture of sand and basalt rock. Marine life abounds in rock pools between the uneven fingers of black basalt which stretch towards the coral reef. At low tide walks can be made to the reef. As the sun dips the rays dancing on the limpid waters have justified the local name of Crystal Basin. All along this coast the sunset is particularly beautiful and pleasant hours can be spent watching well-booted fishermen wading in the shallows. Do take a torch if planning an evening walk.

A lovely coastal drive may be started from Trou aux Biches to Pointe aux Piments. The road cuts inland to Balaclava where the River Citrons flows out into **Baie aux Tortues** (Turtle Bay), named after the great armies of turtles that swam here. None are to be found today but the area is reputed to be the only bay in Mauritius that still contains 90 per cent of live coral. The luxurious Maritime Hotel occupies the site of a summer residence and estate called Balaclava which belonged to a late nineteenth-century Mauritian merchant. Built by the French during Labourdonnais' governorship, the house overlooked the bay and originally formed part of an arsenal where ships and ammunition were supplied for the expeditions to India. Further up the River Citrons was an iron factory and powder mill which in 1774 was blown up by a careless workman causing great loss of life.

Baie aux Tortues can be reached by boats chartered from Grand Baie. Yacht Charters Limited offer an adventurous day of cruising aboard their historic sailing vessel, the *Isla Mauritia*. Built in 1892 she has been faithfully restored and conforms to modern standards with navigation and safety equipment. Complete with Creole crew clad in period uniforms, the *Isla Mauritia* drops anchor at Baie aux Tortues where passengers, after a barbeque at the unspoilt Anse des Filaos beach may explore the underwater life and are entertained to authentic *sega* song and dance and invited to join in the fun.

The vessel will appeal to sailing history buffs. Spanish shipbuilders took 2 years to transform her 90 tons of durable pine into a sailing vessel of lasting elegance and strength. Owned by three generations of the same family she used to sail freight between Europe and Africa until 1959 when she sank in mysterious circumstances. Later she was refloated and registered as a private yacht. In 1988 she completed a successful 6 month trial voyage from Scandinavia to Mauritius.

The sleek lines of the 19m (64ft) catamaran yacht, *Tara*, will appeal to those in search of a modern sea voyage. Tara Charters and Tours at Grand Baie offer a similar route as the *Isla Mauritia* to Baie aux Tortues but with a touch of luxury. Passengers can relax on the wide decks, watch TV/video, snorkel, windsurf, water-ski or scuba dive (a valid scuba-dive certificate must be produced) while the crew prepare cocktails and lunch. With a sail and motor speed both in excess of 15 knots and modern navigational equipment the yacht can accommodate up to thirty-five people although it is available for smaller groups on request.

Tombeau Bay just south of Baie aux Tortues is accessible by road from Balaclava. Cross the bridge over the River Citrons and turn immediately left on to the B41 to connect with the main A4 Triolet-Port Louis road. Nearby are the remains of the powder mill and iron factory of Moulin a Poudre.

At the main road turn right for the bustling little village of **Arsenal** where the inhabitants are fervent supporters of the English football team of the same name. Here a black cannon on a white wall indicates its former importance as an arsenal when the British colonised the island. The road crosses a low bridge over a tranquil lake called Bassin Merven, named after a local who accidentally drove his car into it and drowned.

From here it is 1km ($^1/_2$ mile) through sugar cane fields to **Tombeau Bay** or 'Bay of the Tombs' along the B29. There are fine views of the bay from Le Goulet Snack Bar. In 1615 four ships belonging to the Dutch East Indies Company were caught in a cyclone and ran for the safety of Port Louis. Just a few miles short of their destination they were swept on to the reef at Tombeau Bay. Three ships were wrecked with great loss of life, including Admiral Pieter Both who was on his way home to Holland after a spell as governor of the company. One of Mauritius' most celebrated landmarks is the cup and ball shaped mountain peak to the north of Port Louis which is named after him.

The village of **Baie du Tombeau** straggles along the coast of the B29. Mainly residential with a couple of small hotels, guest houses and rooms for rent, the village is conveniently located for Port Louis and attracts short stay businessmen and visitors from Reunion and the Far East. By day it is a sleepy hideout waking only at night when young folk hungry for the latest offerings in pop music, descend on the Capricorn Discoteque, next door to the Capri Hotel.

Arc-en-Ciel Hotel and restaurant nearby is worth stopping at for

Maheswarnath Temple at Triolet

Big game fishing boats on the north coast

a meal or drink in the spacious dining room overlooking the sea. Popular with Port Louis businessmen at lunchtime the restaurant is renowned for its excellent and extensive Chinese cuisine.

The B29 hugs the coast and then veers inland to meet the Port Louis motorway at Roche Bois. At the roundabout take the first exit marked Pamplemousses in the north to return to Trou aux Biches. A short drive past the Chinese cemetery on the left leads to a second roundabout at Terre Rouge. Take the first exit off the motorway to reach the A4 for Triolet. The road links with Arsenal and the industrial area of Solitude before entering **Triolet.**

The village is the largest in Mauritius with the highest population of Indo-Mauritians many of whom are employed in the tourism and textile sectors. A good bus service links Triolet with the north coast and Port Louis. The village stretches over several miles of pot-holed road where straying pedestrians, dogs and cyclists make for a concentrated drive and save for some beautiful Hindu temples at the far northern end of the village there is little of interest other than watching people go about their business.

Tucked behind the village opposite the Labamba Restaurant, an animated café/restaurant serving Creole and Indian food in the main Triolet road, a one way street leads to an area of several temples. The most beautiful of them is the majestic Maheswarnath Temple built in 1857 which is the largest on the island. No objection is made to photographing the temples but visitors are asked to remove their shoes before entering them.

Opposite the temples is the modern Roman Catholic Church of Notre Dame Des Anges where Mass is held on Saturday and Sunday mornings. To the right of the church is the bus station. From here take the B36 which links with the B38 to return to Trou aux Biches.

Northwards from Trou aux Biches Hotel and before reaching the public beach of Mon Choisy is the Organisation de Peche Du Nord, an independent company offering big game fishing facilities off the north coast. Cabin cruisers equipped with radio equipment and a bilingual crew can be hired for up to several days and programmes can be organised which include a tour of the island and a visit to the private nature reserve of Domaine du Chasseur in the south-east. From the Corsaire Restaurant which forms part of the fishing club there are lovely views across deserted beaches.

At **Mon Choisy** miles of thick forests of filaos trees skirt a brilliant bright beach. A well surfaced road leads past the old landing strip, now a grassy football pitch, where two French pilots, Hily and Surtel, made aviation history in 1933. A monument celebrating the first ever flight from Mauritius indicates that the aircraft travelled 160km (100 miles) to its neighbour, Reunion. The road then reaches the T-junction of the B13 where the left turn leads to Pointe aux Canonniers and Grand Baie through an avenue of flamboyant trees and the right through sugar cane fields towards the A4 Port Louis road.

At this junction there is an imposing walled entrance and gate marked 'Private Property'. The gates are nevertheless open and the driveway shaded by an avenue of coconuts, leads past a delightful colonial residence and the Mon Choisy Farm. The residence is not open to the public but the driveway meanders through the grounds of a former sugar factory where there are the remains of a chimney and windmill. The farm is open to the public for the sale of grain fed poultry, meat and giant prawns.

From the farm a short 1km ($^1/_2$ mile) drive leads to a roundabout. The first exit leads to **Pointe aux Canonniers** (Gunner's Point) where much of the sweeping sandy beach is dominated by Club Mediterranee and Le Canonnier Hotels. The Dutch called the area *De Vuyle Hoek* (Filthy Corner) because so many ships were sunk on the hidden reefs. The French used the headland as a garrison and shore battery and cannons dating back to 1750 can be seen in the tropical gardens of the Canonnier Hotel. The lighthouse, which still stands proud with the remains of the lighthouse keeper's quarters, was a most needful beacon to warn mariners of the dangers of the reef and between 1851 and 1883 alone, twelve shipwrecks were recorded. Under the British it became known as Gunner's Point and it continued to serve as a military post and quarantine area for boats arriving with contagious diseases. A few isolated habitations were built but all that remains is a huge rambling bungalow that was the seaside home of a wealthy Franco-Mauritian family. It still retains the original walls and has been converted into a bar giving superb views of the northern offshore island of Coin de Mire.

The narrow uphill road skirts the Pointe aux Canonniers headland past bougainvillea-bedecked bungalows and the charming Colonial Coconut Hotel where guests are treated to occasional slide shows on the history and culture of Mauritius. The 70-year-old bungalow has been retained and the bamboo clad walls of the dining room and bar are covered in pictures and paintings of its colonial past.

The road descends into the island's most developed resort, **Grand Baie**. It has mushroomed from a quiet little fishing hamlet to a thriving holiday resort. The pace, however, remains slow and easy going yet Grand Baie manages to draw an international clientele to its shores while still retaining a charming village atmosphere. Accommodation ranging from luxurious hotels to cheap pensions and bungalows and well stocked supermarkets and restaurants suit every taste and pocket. The three discoteques attract anyone seeking night life and many restaurants and bars remain open till late.

Local conservationists balk at some of the injudicious building programmes around Grand Baie and the government has banned further development. The fact remains that the resort has a long way to go before it reaches the proportions of mass tourism of Mediterranean hotspots. Shops, boutiques, restaurants, hairdressers, banks, dentists and doctors strung unpretentiously around the bay provides visitors with everything they need.

Grand Baie is the centre for water based activities. Diving, scuba diving, windsurfing, water-skiing, yacht chartering and trips to the northern offshore islands are available from any of the tour operators and diving specialists. Bicycles, motor cycles and cars can be hired and the village is well served by public transport to Port Louis. Occasionally the local Rotary Club organises a 'Fancy Fair', the Mauritiun equivalent of a charity or 'bring and buy' sale on the public beach. They are great opportunities to sample home made snacks or to buy locally produced goods. For these and other local events in the Grand Baie area consult the newspapers or a copy of the monthly *Grand Baie News* which is free and distributed to shops and hotels.

The beach at Grand Baie

Beautiful hand-made models of sailing ships can be viewed at the showrooms of Ceuneau House on the main Choisy-Grand Baie Road. Faithful replicas of famous ships such as the *HMS Victory*, *Cutty Sark* and *Le Superbe* are the result of months of painstaking work. Each model is numbered and a certificate is dedicated to each vessel and its owner. They make unusual souvenirs and can be specially packaged for export. The Ceuneau House showrooms tend to attract an exclusive and knowledgeable clientele and those who are in any doubt as to the authenticity of the materials used are invited to visit the factory at Phoenix.

The art gallery of Helene Senneville nearby holds exhibitions of paintings by Mauritian artists, amongst them Serge Constantin who is the stage director of the Plaza Theatre in Rose Hill and Malcolm de Chazal whose lovely bird and flower paintings can also be admired in public places and hotels. Next door to the gallery is a craft workshop offering wood carvings of fruit and flora.

The work of Mauritian sculptor, Philippe Edwin Marie, may be viewed in a small workshop at the Verandah Bungalow Village Hotel near the Grand Baie Yacht Club. In the Creole village ambience of the hotel he can be seen every day chipping away quietly at dead roots he has collected from river banks.

The Grand Baie Yacht Club sits on a peaceful headland with tranquil views across the bay. Visiting yachtsmen may apply for temporary membership for up to 3 months but are not permitted to invite non-members to the club. The facilities include hot showers, free water from the jetty, reception of mail, rubbish disposal and a bar and snack service.

Next door to the Yacht Club is the Beachcomber owned Royal Palm Hotel. Meals can be taken à la carte in the La Goelette terrace restaurant or in the more private Le Surcouf dining room by arrangement.

Meanwhile the French-owned Pullman Hotel nearby claims not to compete with the Royal Palm but similar sporting and pastime facilities are available together with conference facilities for eighty persons and a French gourmet restaurant.

The B13 coast road follows on to **Pereybèré**, a delightful resort midway between Grand Baie and Cap Malheureux, where vendors sell fruit and snacks from mobile food stalls on the shaded parking area adjacent to the public beach. Unpretentious restaurants within walking distance from the beach serve local, European and Chinese dishes. Independent visitors will find friendly small hotels and self catering/guest house accommodations.

Beyond Pereybèré lies **Cap Malheureux** (Cape of Misfortune) where a large Roman Catholic Church with an orange roof sits on a rocky basalt headland. This is the most northerly point of Mauritius. The island directly opposite is Coin de Mire where a massive British naval force anchored off its shores in 1810, prior to taking control of Mauritius.

There are no shops here but behind the church is an attractive Creole style building of Maison des Pecheurs where self caterers may buy fresh local fish such as *sacre chien, dame berie, veille rouge* and the delicious smoked marlin from the Mauritius Fishermen's Co-operative. It is open every day from 8am-4pm except Sundays.

Near the church there is a neglected cemetery. Follow the rough downhill track which borders it towards the sea. At the end of the track a totally unspoilt basalt and sand beach opens out giving superb views of Coin de Mire. There are a number of private bungalows here and the palatial Creole style residence known as La Maison. Built about 3 years ago, this privately owned property may be rented through local tour operators and comes complete with a team of butlers, maids, cooks and chauffeurs and a crewed luxury catamaran.

To the east of Cap Malheureux Paradise Cove and Grand Gaube Hotels overlook more tranquil beaches notably Anse la Raie and Bain Boeuf where the B13 forms a bridge across an inlet. It zigzags inland through sugar cane fields passing the hamlets of Petit Paquet and St Francois until it reaches the fishing village of **Grand Gaube** (Big Inlet). Residential seaside bungalows are found in this quiet, flat and rather isolated area. The Island View Club Hotel has an ocean view dining area and swimming pool where non guests are welcome.

The road from Grand Gaube turns southwards along the B14 past remains of old sugar factory chimneys and cane fields of the Saint Antoine Sugar Estate to **Goodlands**. This is a busy industrial town with a Sunday market and shops. Of interest is Historic Marine, a model sailing ship factory offering guided tours. The factory started in 1982 with a staff of five making models from copies of original museum plans. Now 350 workers make 40 designs which can take 3 to 5 months to complete. The under structure is made from balsa wood and covered in individual strips of Burmese teak.

From **Poudre d'Or**, an enchanting fishing hamlet on the north-east coast and only 3km (2 miles) from Goodlands, local fishermen make the daily $1^1/_2$ hour passenger crossing to Île d'Ambre and Pointe Bernache. Île d'Ambre was so named because of the ambergris that was supposed to have been found there. These islands make a wonderful day trip for snorkelling, swimming and simple beachcombing in amazingly clear waters. To get to the jetty take the road signposted for the hospital at the staggered junction by Poudre d'Or Police Station.

On the waterfront black basalt rocks stretch out to sea and at low tide the reef where the St Geran was shipwrecked in 1744 can be seen. The vessel was bringing equipment and supplies for the sugar industry. Amongst the passengers were an engaged couple, a Mademoiselle Caillou and a Lieutenant de Montandre who planned to get married. Clinging to a raft the lieutenant pleaded with her to remove her clothes so that they could swim ashore. She refused and instead gave her hand as a token of her love and thanked him for his brave efforts to save her life. The lieutenant then kissed her for the last time and they drowned locked in each others arms. The tragic events inspired eighteenth-century French writer, Bernadin de St Pierre, to write the famous romantic novel, *Paul and Virginie*. The obelisk on the nearby headland was erected 300 years later by the Historical Society of Mauritius to commemorate the sinking. In 1966 the wreck of the St Geran was found by divers and the ship's bell is on display at the Mahebourg Naval Museum.

To the north-west of the obelisk along a narrow road is the colonial built Poudre d'Or Chest Hospital which specialises in chest diseases. Sufferers of tuberculosis benefit from the fresh sea air.

To sample yet more isolated beaches follow the B15 from Poudre d'Or where a small sign on the left indicates Pointe Lascars. Follow this road through sugar cane fields which opens out on to a golden sandy beach. At the end of the beach is a small cemetery and a shelter which was erected by the locals as part of a self help project. The area, was so named because it was popularly believed that Muslim seamen, or the Lascars, from India settled here.

The **Royal Botanical Gardens of Pamplemousses** is the highlight of any visit to the north. Take the B16, which changes its identity to become the A6, from Poudre d'Or via The Mount and turn right on to the A2. If coming from the south along the Port Louis-Mapou motorway take the third exit at the roundabout marked Pamplemousses. The gardens are also well served by bus and taxi from Port Louis.

These world famous gardens were renamed Sir Seewoosagur Ramgoolam Botanical Gardens in 1988 in honour of the late Prime Minister but many locals still refer to them by the former name. Pamplemousses is believed to have taken its name from a citrus plant commonly called the *pamplemoucier* which was imported by the Dutch from Java. The fruit which grows in the area is thick skinned and bitter and resembles a large grapefruit. The Tamils call it the *bambolmas* and it is believed that this is the origin of the French word *pamplemousse* or grapefruit.

Parking is available close to the main entrance gate. The white wrought iron railings and gates won first prize in the International Exhibition in 1862 at Crystal Palace in London but today are rather worn and rusty. Admission is free and touts jostle for business by offering guided tours of dubious content and authenticity. An official guide book by the Conservator of Forests, A.W. Owadally, is on sale at the office inside the gates.

The garden's origins go back to 1735 when Labourdonnais bought a house in the grounds which he called Mon Plaisir. What began as a humble self sufficient vegetable garden developed into a major fresh food source for ships calling at Port Louis. In 1768, Mon Plaisir became the residence of the French intendent and horticulturist, Pierre Poivre who laid the seeds for its present success as a garden of international acclaim. He introduced plants from all over the world and raised indigenous species, the fruits of which can be admired today. They include 80 palms and about 25 species indigenous to the Mascarene Islands, amongst them stately palms, fruit and spice trees, ebony, mahogony, latania and pandanus and occupy some 60 acres of beautiful landscape. Allow at least 2 hours to visit the gardens. Amongst the most impressive sights is the peaceful pond concealed by the enormous floating leaves of the Giant Amazon water lily.

The flowers open white but fade into a dusky pink by the end of the second day. The collection of palms is extensive, amongst them being Royal Palm, Queen Palm from Brazil, Raffia Palms from Madagascar, Lady Palm from China and the Talipot Palm which dies after flowering when it is between 40 and 60 years old.

The Château of Mon Plaisir (dating from around 1850), not to be confused with the original Mon Plaisir, is a two storeyed English–built mansion with high ceilings and wood panelling overlooking Sir John Pope Hennessy Avenue. The interior has decayed slightly and the plain walls are devoid of interest. However from the ground floor verandah superb views of the Moka range and the unmistakable peak of Pieter Both can be photographed. The ground floor is now used as a reception area for distinguished visitors.

A reconstruction of an early sugar mill stands between the château and the Tortoise Pen. Oxen used to crush the cane by rotating vertical cyclinders to extract the juice which was heated and left to crystallise.

The oldest residents of the gardens are the giant Aldabra tortoises imported from the island of the same name in the Seychelles Archipelago. The first arrivals took place in 1875 at the request of the Royal

Society of Arts and Sciences as it was feared they would become extinct in Aldabra. Wholesale slaughter of the creatures began in the eighteenth century when sailors and colonists butchered them for their meat and liver. Some 13,000 tortoises were shipped to Mauritius and elsewhere in a 5 year period towards the end of the eighteenth century. By the end of the nineteenth century the tortoise was a protected species in Aldabra. Charles Darwin took a leading part in the movement to preserve it. Now Aldabra is the only place in the world where it proliferates. The secret to their longevity is an unhurried, unrushed lifestyle — something to remember when sightseeing.

Animal lovers will appreciate the fauna of the gardens. There is a small deer compound off Plaisir Avenue where descendants of the deer imported from Indonesia by the Dutch in 1639 can be admired. The red billed Madagascar Moorhen inhabits a small lake called Grand Bassin. Here several inaccessible islets covered with papyrus, badamier and ravenala are a sanctuary for other birds and large goldfish called Dame Cere share the waters alongside other species from Africa, India and Central America. Birds, bats and non venomous small reptiles from the Mascarenes and further afield roam free in the tropical lushness.

The basalt built Church of St François just outside the main gate, is the oldest Catholic church in Mauritius. It was built in 1756 and named in honour of Labourdonnais. Some of the islands oldest graves are in the cemetery, amongst them Abbe Buonavita who was Napoleon's almoner while he was in exile in St Helena and Adrien d'Epinay, founder of *La Cerneen Newspaper*, whose body was returned to Mauritius from France in 1840. Epinay bought Mon Plaisir after Poivre and introduced many exotic plants.

Return to the roundabout on the Port Louis-Mapou motorway where the lovely grounds of Beau Plan Sugar Estate are situated. Nearby is the Sir Seewoosagur Ramgoolam National Hospital, where English speaking staff provide excellent treatment. Just beyond the hospital on the junction of the B18 and B11, concealed in thick woodland, is a monument,to the Singhalese prince, Ehelepola, who was exiled by the British to Mauritius for plotting to overthrow them in Ceylon in 1825. He died in Mauritius 3 years later.

From Pamplemousses roundabout it is only 5km (3 miles) along the A5 northwards to **Mapou** where the Sir Aneerood Jugnath Sports Stadium is situated. Completed in 1990 with Chinese aid at a cost of about 100 million rupees, it is the most modern sports stadium in the Indian Ocean with 11,100 seats and standing room for 25,000.

Alternatively a scenic drive may be made to **La Nicolière Reser-**

voir and mountains by taking the A2 from Pamplemousses via The Mount and Grand Rosalie. The Château of Grand Rosalie, built in the mid-eighteenth century by the French Governor Villebague, occupies land on the islands first sugar estate. It is fenced off and not open to the public. Good but distant views of the château surrounded by rolling landscape may be had by continuing along the A2 in the direction of Villebague and taking the signposted road for La Nicolière on the right before entering the village. The road meanders uphill through sugar cane fields to the high banks of La Nicolière Reservoir which was built in the 1920s to irrigate the northern plains. The road zigzags through some of the loveliest wooded areas of Mauritius eventually linking with the B49 to St Pierre to the south of the Port Louis mountains. Allow plenty of time for the journey south from La Nicolière along pot holed roads.

Northern Offshore Islands

These formed as a result of early volcanic explosions from the centre of Mauritius and with the exception of Île d'Ambre are designated nature reserves. Landing requires a permit from the Conservator of Forests at Curepipe.

From west to east the first and closest island is **Coin de Mire** which is composed of layers of crumbling volcanic sandstone. From the air it looks like a massive turtle yet from the coast at Cap Malheureux it takes on the appearance of an enormous wedge of cheese.

Next comes **Flat Island** fringed by coral reef to the east which completely encircles its neighbour, **Gabriel Island** and endows it with its own lagoon. They were conveniently distanced from Mauritius to serve as quarantine stations during the mid-nineteenth century when cholera imported from India almost wiped out the population of Port Louis. The cemetery on the east coast of Flat Island stands as a lonely reminder to the number of victims. Both islands are uninhabited but trips to the lighthouse on Flat Island depending on weather conditions, can be made through tour operators in Grand Baie. To the north of Flat Island is an uninhabited rock called Le Pigeonnier (Pigeon House Rock).

Round Island, which is not round but a semi spherical mound of rock, lies further to the east. A hostile coastline and strong currents make landing dangerous and for this reason endemic species of flora and fauna have been able to survive through centuries without human interference. The island, a bare and barren haystack rising from the sea, is the habitat of the rare Telfair Skink which resembles a flattened lizard, geckos and two species of snakes all of whom live happily alongside the tropic bird (*paille en queue* — the bird on the Air Mauritius emblem). Organised boat and helicopter trips through tour operators in Grand Baie are available. Circular Serpent Island, north of Round Island is inhabited by thousands of birds, not snakes.

Day excursions with picnic lunch to Île d'Ambre in the north-east and Pointe Bernache can be arranged from Grand Baie or with local fishermen at Poudre d'Or.

Additional Information

Goodlands
Historic Marine
Z.I. De St Antoine
☎ 283 9304
Open: Monday to Friday 8am-5pm
and Saturdays 8am-12noon.

Grand Baie
Ceuneau House
☎ 263 7849
Open: Monday to Friday 10am-8pm,
Saturdays 8am-12noon.

*Helen Senneville Art Gallery and
    Workshop*
Route Royal
☎ 263 7426
Open: Monday to Friday, 9.30am-
5pm.

*Verandah Bungalow Village Hotel
    Workshop*
Between the Pullman Hotel and
Grand Baie Yacht Club
☎ 263 8015
Open: Monday to Friday 9 30am-4pm.

Mon Choisy
Farm Shop
Open: Monday to Friday 8.30-11am
and 12noon-3.30pm. Saturdays
8.30-11am.

Pamplemousses
*Royal Botanical Gardens of
    Pamplemousses*
Open: daily from 6am-6pm.
Admission free.
Public toilets, seating areas.

If you wish to visit the Beau Plan
sugar factory then contact the
Public Relations Officer
Beau Plan
Pamplemousses
☎ 3 3544

Trou aux Biches
Aquarium
Coast Road
☎ 261 6187
Open: every day, including public
holidays, 9am-5pm.

Argonaute Shell Museum and Shop
Coast Road
☎ 261 6176
Open: Monday to Friday, 9am-5 30,
Saturday 9am-12noon.

Tourist information and car hire is
available at all hotels and travel
agents.

2
THE EAST COAST

The east coast from Pointe de Roches Noires to Mahebourg is relatively isolated and public transport from hotels and accommodation is virtually non-existent. Visitors must rely on taxis or hire cars if they wish to explore the island but the east has some lovely scenery with wonderful views of the Grand Port mountain range. From north to south they rise from a sea of sugar cane to form the peaks of the Blanche, Bambou and Creole mountains. The trade winds dominate the entire coast bringing cooling breezes throughout the hot summer months and strong bracing winds during winter.

Much of the land is owned by FUEL (Flacq United Estates Limited), the largest sugar estate in Mauritius, and the smaller sugar estates of Constance, Beau Champ and Riche en Eau. Large areas of sugar cane are often interlined with plots of onions, tomatoes, chillies, peanuts and aubergines for local consumption.

Because of the east coast's isolation the hotels provide excellent accommodation and facilities. Most occupy great stretches of white beaches with idyllic lagoons while small tourist shops and mini markets near self catering bungalows provide the perfect setting for relaxing holidays but the area is impregnated with history, particularly around Mahebourg. Driving on badly made roads requires stamina, but organised sightseeing tours are available from hotels.

Mahebourg excluded, the area lies in the district of Flacq. It is flanked by Plaine des Roches in the north and the Bambou Mountains in the south. Wonderfully scenic drives may be experienced either by hire car, taxi or bus. Those staying at or near St Geran or Belle Mare Plage hotels are advised to commence their journeys from Centre de Flacq, the main town of the administrative district of Flacq.

Centre de Flacq is a small lively town with higgledy-piggledy shops, banks, pharmacies, doctors, dentists, food stalls and a daily

50

The East Coast • 51

market providing those on the east coast with everything they need.

The town has good bus links with Curepipe. Rose Hill and Port Louis, and provides services, albeit irregular, to the smaller coastal villages of Trou d'Eau Douce in the south to Poudre d'Or in the north. A one-way system of traffic operates through the town where there is a market and taxi stand. Next to the market is the large late nineteenth-century basalt built District Court House. Listed as a National Monument, the District Court House made history in May 1990 when one of Mauritius' top politicians, Sir Gaetan Duval, was committed to the Supreme Court to stand trial on a charge of conspiracy to murder. Attention was focused on the town when hundreds of his supporters and well-wishers turned up at the court. The charge was subsequently dismissed.

The building is the Civil Status Office (the equivalent to a Register Office) where foreign holidaymakers wishing to get married must attend prior to the delightful wedding ceremonies which are performed on the beach of luxury class hotels.

Centre de Flacq gives easy access to the lovely coast of Roches Noires and Poste Lafayette in the north. Leave the centre of town via the A7 to link with the B23 where a right turn leads to the hamlet of Poste de Flacq. At the crossroads there is a delightful little tourist café-cum-souvenir shop called Imagine where drinks are served on a patio. (A sign indicating right for St Geran Hotel is situated at this crossroads but visitors should avoid using this road. It is very badly surfaced and they are advised to drive via Centre de Flacq instead).

The B15 to the left of this junction passes through neat thick forests of filao trees to Poste Lafayette and provides wonderful shady vistas and glimpses of translucent blue seas. Inland lies the flatlands of Plaine des Roches, with its conical mounds of black volcanic rocks and boulders protruding from the green cane fields. An airport was planned here but numerous caves were found, making it unsuitable.

Buses from Centre de Flacq operate along this stretch of isolated coast as far as Poudre d'Or and Goodlands in the north. Buses stop outside the Kestrel Hotel which is 5km (3 miles) from Poste de Flacq. It makes a pleasant stop where refreshments can be taken overlooking the bay across the peninsular of Pointe d'Esny. The Racing Club of Mauritius, is almost adjacent to the Kestrel Hotel. Tourists are welcome to use the premises, which include a bar, during the day as long as no club activities are in progress.

One hundred metres beyond the Kestrel Hotel on the coast side is a horse riding stable called Horse Haven run by an animal-loving English lady. She opened the stables in 1988 after learning that injured ex-racing horses were to be put down. Following careful

The East Coast • 53

nursing the horses were brought back to health and are available for hire by the half day to experienced riders only. In summer the heat is too intense for the horses and riding is confined to the cooler temperatures of the morning or late afternoon. Reservations should be made 2 days before the ride and confirmed the day before through Mrs Marion Bouic ☎ 283 9322 or through the Kestrel Hotel ☎ 283 9336.

Half a kilometre after Horse Haven and just before a football pitch there is access to a wild and windy beach studded with black rocks. Here a monument is erected to the memory of five soldiers of the Special Mobile Force (the Mauritian para military police) who drowned at sea on 9 July 1964 following training exercises. The upright monument stands isolated against a backdrop of rough and dangerous sea reminding all who pass this way that Mauritius is not all limpid lagoons. Each year in July a pilgrimage is made to the monument by SMF colleagues.

From Roches Noires the B15 continues to the A6 veering inland to the bridge over the Rivière du Rempart to reach the busy town of the same name. Bus connections with Pamplemousses and Port Louis and the open-air market provide daily needs. Beyond town are the neat grounds and sugar factory of Mon Loisir. To return to Centre de Flacq continue along the A6 and turn left at Belle Vue Maurel on to the B22 for views of the enormous Plaine des Roches and the sugar cane plantations of Constance Sugar Estate.

Centre de Flacq is also a convenient departure point to visit the village of **Quatre Cocos** in the south. Take the B61 heading east from the bus station towards Belle Mare. The road sweeps through undulating fields of sugar cane for 2km (1 mile) until a sign indicates left for Mare La Chaux and Belle Mare and straight on the Quatre Cocos and Palmar, $2^1/_2$km ($1^1/_2$ miles) later a sign indicates Quatre Cocos Government School on the left. The road is quaintly named Quatre Cocos High Street.

The village received a face-lift preceding the official visit of the Duke and Duchess of York in 1987 when 'Welcome to the Village' signs were erected and garden walls were re-painted blue and white. Today bougainvillea and hibiscus cascade over the picturesquely decayed walls and signs imploring all to keep the village clean are reminiscent of an English village in the tropics. At the Health Centre a flower-bedecked driveway leads to the white stucco building of the Cultural and Handicraft Centre where a plaque commemorates its official opening by the Duke and Duchess of York. Sadly it no longer operates as a cultural centre and the small theatre and adjacent workrooms remain empty and unused save for the efforts of one small private business called Quatre Cocos Ceramics Limited who offer for sale items of locally made pottery.

Belle Mare village and public beach lie 1km ($^1/_2$ mile) to the north-east of Quatre Cocos through sugar cane fields and the marshlands of Mare du Puit and Mare aux Trois Ilots. Beyond the village at a three way junction three colourful Hindu gods squat like giant garden gnomes on neat lawns. Across the road a modern glass fronted shop called Galeries Baulwen sells model ships and souvenirs.

The public beach is white and clean and fringed by filao trees. It is one of the least crowded since there is no bus service. However driveways meander through the filao trees and there is parking space, public toilets, picnic areas and refreshment kiosks. The remains of old kilns testify to the former industry of coral burning. A staircase encircles one of these kilns and provides lovely viewpoints of the coast and countryside.

Nearby is a marble cenotaph erected in memory of 159 passengers and crew who died following a plane crash at sea. The Helderburg, a 747 combi-plane belonging to South African Airways, crashed in unexplained circumstances en route from Taipei to Mauritius on 28 November 1987. The wreckage was recovered just off the east coast. A pilgrimage here is organised each year by South African Airways.

Continuing south along the B59 from Belle Mare beach the road is bordered by thick and varied vegetation and is at times close to the shore. Rest at the beach at **Palmar** if only to admire its tranquil turquoise lagoon. The Hotel Ambre and Tropical Hotel are hidden amongst thick vegetation a few kilometres on and makes a welcome stop where there are stupendous views across the lagoon to Île de l'Est and Touessrok and the peaks of the Bambou Mountains.

The B59 to Trou d' Eau Douce and its superb beaches requires calm concentration to negotiate the potholes and for comfort speeds of 50kph (31mph) cannot be exeeded. **Trou d'Eau Douce**, one of the first Dutch settlements means 'the hole of sweet water' and is named after the abundance of fresh water springs in the area.

On entering the village there is a fuel station and three small restaurants, La Cambuse, Chez Tino and La Caze la Paille, all serving Creole and European food and catering for tourists and locals. These are the last watering holes before reaching Touessrok Hotel and Île aux Cerfs. The village is a maze of narrow streets where colourful washing is haphazardly strewn over walls of tumbledown dwellings. Nearby is the renovated Roman Catholic Church of Our Lady of Good and Perpetual Succour.

South on the B59 a good road leads to the entrance of the Touessrok Hotel. It is bordered with great bushes of bougainvillea and speed ramps deter any driver who might be in a hurry. The reception area is on the mainland but the activities and accommodations are sited on a small sandy island across a Venetian-style wooden footbridge. In 1988 the Duke and Duchess of York stayed in the hotel's presidential suite overlooking Île aux Cerfs. The hotel, located in one of the most exotic locations in Mauritius, specialises in wedding ceremonies on the beach and its isolation may appeal to honeymooners.

Île aux Cerfs (Stag Island) nearly opposite Touessrok comprises 700 acres (280 hectares) of luxuriant woodland where deer roam wild. It has excellent beaches for swimming and snorkelling and the shallow lagoon is particularly safe for children. It takes about 3 hours to walk round of the island but visitors are advised not to stray off the marked paths. The northern tip is reserved for public facilities and include first aid post, showers, toilets, shops and a boat house for watersports and boat trips. There is a tortoise and deer pen.

Boats to Île aux Cerfs are available free of charge for guests staying at Touessrok Hotel. Public services operate from the jetty at Pointe Maurice via gardens off to the right of the main approach road of Touessrok. The crossing takes about 20 minutes and motorists may leave vehicles in the shaded free parking area. Boats leave every half hour from 9am to 5pm. Staying overnight and picnicking are prohib-

Domaine du Chasseur nature reserve

ited but refreshment is available from the hotel managed beach bar and restaurants. La Chaumiere offers Creole dishes while exotic Paul and Virginie Restaurant specialises in seafood. The boathouse hires out windsurf boards and water-skis and enjoyable trips can be made in the lagoon in glass bottom boats.

Dinghies from Île aux Cerfs or Pointe Maurice go to the longest river in Mauritius, Grand River South East (Grand Rivière Sud Est). It springs from the Piton du Milieu in the centre of the island and flows down the western flank of the Bambou Mountains. It terminates 40km (25 miles) later at the cascading waterfalls at Beau Champ. Experienced boatmen ferry tourists to the dark and deep estuary where the river runs fast over boulders and rocks. Black shiny basalt cliffs bathed by a rush of waterfall are where young boys keen to provide tourists with entertainment in exchange for a few rupees or cigarettes, dive head first into the clear waters and emerge to scale the rocks and start all over again.

A drive from Trou d'Eau Douce via Bel Air to Mahebourg is one of the loveliest excursions of the east coast. The road sweeps through untidy but picturesque Indian villages with temples and mosques standing alongside each other and tranquil fishing hamlets where dark Creole fishermen wade in the shallow lagoons. In places the road runs parallel with the ocean giving panoramic views of the islets off Mahebourg.

From Touessrok Hotel follow the road inland to the mysteriously named junction of Sept Chemins (Seven Streets) where actually six small roads converge to form the B59 running southwards from Trou d'Eau Douce. Turn left on the B59 for Bel Air where a sign indicates Plaisance Airport. The B59 snakes its way through sugar cane fields until it crosses the Rivière Seche and reaches Bel Air. At Bel Air turn left on to the B28, or the Old Coast Road, for Mahebourg.

Tall coconut trees herald the entrance to Beau Champ Sugar Estate 3km (2 miles) on the left along the B28 from Bel Air. A detour may be made to visit the east banks of the Grand River South East and the village of the same name, along a rough road.

Continuing along the B28 the road crosses several narrow bridges over the Grand River South East before reaching the wider 1970s built Beau Champ Bridge which is surrounded by lovely views. The road then drops downhill and a steep embankment hides the river from view. Three kilometres (2 miles) southwards along the B28 is the hamlet of **Deux Frères** (Two Brothers) on the west bank, named after two hills of similar appearance, from where, subject to local demand, a free ferry ride crosses the river.

The next hamlet is **Quatre Soeurs** (Four Sisters) and here the winding road is badly surfaced. Following the shoreline, it barely manages to keep a toehold on land as it contrives to avoid the steep foothills of the towering Bambou Mountains. The villages of **Grand Sable** and **Petit Sable** sit at each end of a wide unprotected bay. Petit Sable has a rather unattractive beach. Out to sea are the islets of **Île aux Oiseaux** and **Îlot Flamants.**

At **Pointe du Diable** (Devil's Point) motorists can park on a grassy headland where there are eighteenth-century ruins of French batteries. The walls with narrow observation slits are over 2m (7ft) thick and cannons dating back to 1750 face seaward. Built originally to guard the entrance to the reefs there are fine views of Île aux Fouquets with its lighthouse and the sprinkling of islands just inside the reef. Early navigators sailing past the headland attributed the illogical readings of their compasses to the devil.

Soil erosion has discoloured the sea and the coastline is not particularly attractive although inland the Bambou Mountains provide a dramatic backdrop through the villages of Bamboux Virieux and Pointe Bamboux.

Anse Jonchée, 5km (3 miles) after Pointe du Diable, is a sweeping bay with calm waters. A large sign indicates **Domaine du Chasseur** inland. It is worth visiting this private nature reserve either independently or with a tour. A track winds uphill through sugar cane clad slopes to an altitude of 300m (984ft) with outstanding views of the reef and islands where the 1810 sea battle of Grand Port took place. Formerly private hunting and shooting parties travelled from the towns to spend weekends here. Since 1988 the area has been developed for tourism.

Deer and game shoots can be organised with experienced guides in robust vehicles equipped with radio. The management claim to own 1,500 deer, 500 wild boar, monkey, rabbit and hare in the 400 acres (160 hectares) of protected land. Six safari style bungalows are perched on a steep slope overlooking an open thatched bar which serves snacks and drinks. The restaurant has individual tables cunningly terraced along the hillside giving the impression of dining in the tree tops. The menu offers unusual Mauritian dishes such as venison curry, grilled lobsters, roasted wild pig, fresh fish and *salade coeur de palmiste* (heart of palm salad). It is also known as 'millionaires salad' because it takes 7 years for the palm to mature.

The area is the habitat of the endangered Mauritius Kestrel. Following the use of pesticides the kestrel virtually disappeared from the Bambou Mountains in the 1940s. A breeding programme to raise young kestrels in captivity for releasing into the wild was introduced in the 1970s with great success. Each afternoon they appear much to the delight of camera clicking tourists and wildlife enthusiasts who watch them swoop down on offerings of dead mice supplied by a representative of the Black River Aviary.

Steep paths, some at 45° and bounded by wooded areas of ebony, olive, bergamot, cinammon and travellers palms attract the hillwalker and nature lover. The less energetic can be ferried on a bone jerking safari trip along rough bumpy paths to the summit with a helicopter landing pad and panoramic vistas of sea and mountain.

Admission charge includes services of a vehicle. Advance bookings for accommodation or hunting parties should be made on ☎ 631 9259. Bungalow and hunting charges are available at the kiosk.

Bois des Amourettes (Woods of the Young Lovers) is 3km (2 miles) on from Anse Jonchée. The woodlands, now clothed with sugar cane, were frequented by French soldiers from the garrison at Mahebourg and their sweethearts. During World War II the British established a naval look-out post but all that remains are some old concrete bunkers poking through the cane fields on the seashore.

The police station, a 1960s built concrete style building set slightly inland, marks the beginning of the village of **Vieux Grand Port**. From here to Mahebourg the road is impregnated with the history of the first Dutch settlers. In the village, is the 1958 built Roman Catholic Church of Notre Dame de Grand Pouvoir. The grounds sweep down to the sea where a green and white pavilion overlooks Grand Port Bay. Along the water's edge are the caves of Salles d'Armes where gentlemen fought duels. As the caves are only accessible by sea it is best to go with a knowledgeable fisherman.

To the right of the church are the disintegrating and blackened walls of Fort Frederick Henry. They are in fact the remains of French buildings built on the site of the original Dutch settlement. The Dutch arrived in 1598 but several attempts at colonisation ended in failure and they eventually abandoned the island in 1710. The French demolished the ruins in 1753 and used the materials to construct new headquarters for their garrison at Mahebourg.

The road continues through Vieux Grand Port which under the Dutch, was called Warwyck Bay. The French renamed it Port Bourbon in 1722 and it became the headquarters of the French East India Company. The entrance to the port, however, was open to fierce south-east trade winds and 5 years later the capital was transferred to Port Louis, with a much safer harbour. Meanwhile Port Bourbon was renamed Port Sud Est and lost much of its importance until a new town was built in the south of the bay in 1805. It was called Mahebourg in honour of Mahe de Labourdonnais.

It is only a short drive from Vieux Grand Port to **Ferney** where there is a magnificent white Creole residence belonging to the sugar factory of the same name. It is closed to the public but its spacious gardens reflect the grandeur of former times and can be viewed from the gates. Ferney was one of the first sugar estates established by the French in 1743. At the entrance of a shaded driveway leading to the sugar factory there is a monument erected by the Mauritian Societe des Chasseurs. It commemorates the landing of the Dutch Governor, Adriaan Van der Stel, aboard the *Capelle* ship from Java on 8 November 1639 laden with deer to supply the Dutch settlers with fresh meat. Deer farming today is an important agricultural activity.

Shortly after crossing the Ferney Bridge across the River Nyon, another monument erected in 1953, commemorates the introduction of sugar to Mauritius again by Governor Van der Stel in 1639.

The B28 continues and just before a concrete bridge across the River Champagne there is a small white house on the left. A narrow pathway to the rear leads to a jetty where an obelisk commemorates the first Dutch landing in 1598 under Admiral Van Warwyck.

From Ferney it is 5km (3 miles) to Mahebourg. It lies on the southern shores of the immense Vieux Grand Port Bay with views of Lion Mountain to the north. The B28 crosses the River des Creoles

Wash day by the River des Creoles

where sari-swathed Indian women, knee-deep in water, wash great bundles of laundry and spread it out to dry on the river banks.

North of Mahebourg is **Ville Noire**, named after the black slaves who arrived in appalling conditions from Africa and Madagascar. It is really an extension of Mahebourg linked by the British built Cavendish Bridge over the River La Chaux. Dutch, French and English settlers have left their influence on this river by naming it Limoen, Citronniers and Lime River respectively. Its present name, 'Chaux' is a French translation of 'lime'. At the turn of the century there were numerous lime kilns in Mauritius. Coral was burnt in them and the lime extracted from it was used for building materials. Mahebourg has one of the last remaining operational lime kilns.

❄ Under the French, **Mahebourg** was a busy, thriving port town. The British, realising its importance, linked it to Port Louis by rail. The service stopped in 1964 and the former railway station on the waterfront which now houses administrative buildings. Mahebourg remains an important village in spite of it having lost much of its former elegance although its busy bus station, taxi stand, shops and market give it the appearance of a small town. It has a laid back atmosphere with several guest houses and snack bars. Mahebourg is a fine example of the island's religious and racial harmony reflected by a Hindu and Telegu temple, a mosque, a Roman Catholic church, an Anglican church and several shrines venerated by all denominations to Pere Laval and St Antoine de Padoue, dotted around the village and all within walking distance of each other.

The village, with tumbledown garden walls dating back to the eighteenth century, is neatly laid out in grid style with street names reflecting the influence of European settlers. In the centre of the village beneath a red corrugated roofed building the lively market displays exotic fruit, vegetables, herbs and spices each day. On Mondays, people converge in the streets to sell household goods, clothing, and material. In Route Royale there is a branch of the Mauritius Commercial Bank.

Mahebourg is renowned for its 'biscuits manioc'. The ramshackle factory, the oldest in Mauritius, is situated in Ville Noire. Cross the Cavendish Bridge and turn left at the sign marked 'Old Coast Road'.
❄ The road twists and turns until it reaches the factory. The biscuits are made from manioc or the cassava root and used to be the only biscuits ever produced in Mauritius. Today they can be bought in most supermarkets and are particularly good with cheese. The makers, the long established Mauritian Rault family, received a silver award at an exhibition in London in 1908. Visits are possible by calling at the factory.

At Pointe des Regattes is a monument to the French and English who died in the 1810 Battle of Grand Port. The battle lasted several days and was a great attempt by the British to conquer the island. It ended in defeat for the British and both sides suffered heavy casualties. The French victory is inscribed on the Arc de Triomphe in Paris.

The fascinating aspects of this battle can be seen in the Historical and Naval Museum of Mahebourg, a dilapidated colonial residence built in around 1771 that belonged to the Commandant of the District of Grand Port, Jean de Robillard. His initials are inscribed on the wrought iron balustrade of the house. After the Battle of Grand Port, De Robillard turned the house into a hospital and the commanders of the French and British forces, Rear Admiral Victor Duperre and Admiral Sir Nesbit Willoughby, convalesced alongside each other and no doubt sobered by the appaling loss of men and ships, shook hands symbolising the beginning of an *entente cordiale*.

The house was bought by the government in 1950 and turned into a museum under the direction of the Mauritius Institute. It is at the southern outskirts of the village on the Mahebourg-Curepipe road.

The museum occupies three floors, two of which are accessible to the public. On the ground floor wreckage of sailing ships that took part in the Grand Port battle, original cannon, cannonball, paintings and swords and weaponry of Robert Surcouf, the eighteenth-century corsair, popularly known as the King of the Corsairs. A large relief map shows the complicated reefs of Vieux Grand Port where the great battle took place. The bell, recovered from the wreckage of the *St Geran* which sunk off the east coast in 1744, is also on display. There is an interesting newspaper cutting of Charles Seabourne, who with survivors from the ship *Trevessa*, landed at Bel Ombre in the south in 1923 after spending 25 days at sea. On display are the ship's biscuits, a razor and the lid of a cigarette tin which they used to measure water rations. In a separate showcase is a Roll of Honour dedicated to Mauritians who died in World War II.

On the first floor are Labourdonnais' four-poster bed, two palanquins or wooden sedan-type chairs, which were borne by slaves to convey their masters through the country and a collection of coins, curios, model sailing ships and early maps, labelled in French and English.

Unfortunately the richness of its collection does not reflect the grandeur of the house. The museum lies in neglected grounds and is in need of renovation. Behind the museum is a rusty railway carriage that belonged to the British governors. In its heyday it was luxuriously appointed and continued to be so even after its relegation to a funeral carriage that transported corpses for burial around the island. With the demise of the railway line the carriage served as an office for the Conservator of Forests before its final journey to doom and neglect.

It is pleasant strolling around Mahebourg. At the weekend families picnic on the grassy verges of Pointe des Regattes. Cheap and cheerful accommodation and simple restaurants overlooking the sea contrast with the more conventional amenities of the established tourist track. Just across the water is the picturesque islet of **Mouchoir Rouge** whose only dwelling is the red-roofed bungalow of the official caretaker.

At Swami Sivanandah Street, just behind the waterfront heading south towards Blue Bay, is the charming Le Vacancier Hotel and Restaurant where Mauritian cuisine is served by friendly staff in a rustic setting. Nearby are the Sea Fever and Monte Carlo Guest Houses which are popular with Reunionese visitors. Bicycles can be hired from the Crysanthemum Handicraft Shop next door.

The road merges with Labourdonnais Street heading out of the village past the lawns in front of the ugly Emmanuel Anquetil Secondary School where there is a boat-shaped concrete monument to journalist and representative of the coloured population, Remy Ollier who was born in 1816 at nearby Ferney.

At Pointe Jerome is the well-run Croix du Sud Hotel, with *sega* dancing shows and nightly entertainment. Tours of the coast and visits to Île aux Aigrettes, opposite the hotel, can be made from the boat house. The journey takes about 20 minutes.

Île aux Aigrettes (Egret Island), rises a mere 9m (30ft) and covers an area of 59 acres (24 hectares) of dense shrub. Illegal woodcutters over the years have denuded what was left of its trees and it is now a designated nature reserve. The road passes through the attractive residential area of colonial style bungalows of Pointe d'Esny and terminates at the public beach of Blue Bay. Some bungalows for rent are advertised in the local press and bed and breakfast is available.

❄ At **Blue Bay** the bluest of calm waters separates the tiny Île des Deux Cocos (Island of Two Coconuts) from the mainland and midweek it is a paradise for sunlovers and beachcombers. Sparkling beaches, filao trees, picnic areas, public toilets, showers and the Blue Bay Tuck Shop attract locals from all over the island at weekends and public holidays making it an opportunity to experience a slice of Mauritian beach life.

❄ An interesting side trip may be made from Mahebourg to **Le Val Nature Park**, which forms part of the only government-owned sugar estate in Mauritius, the 7,000-acre (2,800-hectare) Rose Belle Sugar Estate. Take the B7 from Ville Noire to the village of **Riche en Eau** on

Taking a dip at one of Mahebourg's top-class hotels

Market day at Mahebourg

the banks of the River des Creoles. The area, meaning literally 'rich in water', contained many family owned sugar estates and today it is dominated by the huge modern sugar factory of Riche en Eau. The road winds northwards to Cent Gaulettes and Le Val where isolated chimneys mark the place of these early sugar factories and the remains of buildings or 'habitations' in which families lived. These chimneys, some sprouting trees and shrubs, are listed as 'National Monuments.'

Le Val is an example of how sugar estates are diversifying into agriculture and farming activities. Here freshwater prawns of the Rosenberghi variety are specially bred in chemically treated water. Anthuriums thrive in greenhouses for export and huge plots of watercress and *brede songe* (edible greens) are grown for home consumption. There is an enclosure of deer and sheep wander freely along the banks and bamboo bridges of tranquil streams. There are some exotic palms, amongst them the Terminalia Tree from Madagascar, public toilets, open-air kiosks and a mini aquarium housing some eels and tropical fish. There are no guides or refreshment facilities and visitors, not accompanied by a tour operator, are left to their own devices.

It is possible to combine a visit to Le Val with a shopping trip to Curepipe by heading for Cluny on the B83. Here turn right to join the A10 Nouvelle France-Curepipe road. The route from Curepipe to Le Val is described in the Excursions from Curepipe section.

Additional Information

Centre de Flacq
District Court House
Open: Monday to Friday, 10am-4pm. Public gallery available for listening to court cases.

Mahebourg
Historical and Naval Museum of Mahebourg
Open: Monday, Wednesday, Friday and Saturday 9am-4pm. Closed Tuesday, Thursday, Sunday and public holidays.
No photography.
Admission free.

Manioc Biscuit Factory (Rault/ Senneque)
Les Delices
☎ 631 9559
Open: erratic opening hours but visits may be made by calling in person.

Le Val Nature Park
☎ through Rose Belle Sugar Estate 627 4545
Open: Monday to Friday 9am-4pm. Admission charge.

Tourist information and car hire is available at all hotels and travel agents.

3

THE SOUTH COAST

The rugged south coast stretching eastwards from Baie du Cap to Blue Bay is often overlooked by visitors. Nevertheless the lack of accommodation and safe beaches seem to attract the curious and adventurous traveller to experience a world far removed from the luxury hotel resorts of the north. The south humbly apologises for its lack of touristic amenities yet compensates by offering breathtaking scenery and a feeling of going back in time. Great stretches of black basalt cliffs assaulted by the strong south-easterly winds contrasting with a backdrop of undulating hills and dales of sugar cane, rivers and forests confuse the reality of being on a tropical island and Mauritians will tell you, sooner or later, that the south was how Mauritius used to be.

Rivers flowing from the central uplands into the sea have, in many places, prevented coral reefs from gaining a foothold, depriving the area of the gentle lagoons reminiscent of the north and swimming, except from designated beaches, can be dangerous. In the west the Savanne Mountains rise steeply from deep coves relegating the road to a narrow strip which hugs the seashore to Souillac. The east is flatter and roads link small shanty villages and towns through sugar cane fields with bridges crossing many rivers and streams. The area lies in the districts of Savanne and Grand Port where the sugar estates of Bel Ombre, St Felix, Union Saint Aubin, Britannia, Savannah and Mon Tresor Mon Desert own and cultivate much of the land.

With access from Le Morne, Curepipe and Mahebourg, the south coast can be visited in a day. Regular bus services cover the coast from Baie du Cap to Souillac and the inland villages of Chemin Grenier, Surinam, Rivière des Anguilles, L'Escalier and Plaine Magnien. ' Taxi trains' or communal taxis supplement the bus route providing fast cheap travel.

66 • Visitor's Guide: Mauritius, Rodrigues & Reunion

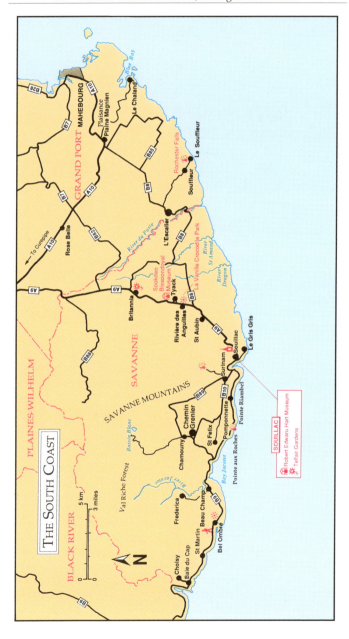

The South Coast • 67

The only main road from Baie du Cap to Souillac is the B9. **Baie du Cap** is a small coastal village which depends on fishing and agriculture and is typical of many on the south coast with a few Chinese-run stores, a police station, post office, school and community centre. An office of the National Coastguard marks the end of the village.

Just before reaching Bel Ombre about 4km (2 miles) to the east of Baie du Cap a monument on the coast side near St Martin's Cemetery marks the place where Charles Seabourne and sixteen survivors landed in 1923 when their ship, the *Trevessa*, foundered 1,610 miles (998km) off the coast of Mauritius. The ship was on its way from Australia when the crew abandoned it drifting in two lifeboats for 25 days before reaching Mauritius. One lifeboat reached Rodrigues and the other reached Bel Ombre 3 days later. Eight members of the crew died at sea and one died a day after landing in Mauritius.

An avenue of lofty coconut trees heralds the approach to the sugar factory of **Bel Ombre** (Beautiful Shadows). The estate lies in 15,000 acres (6,000 hectares) of undulating land with a unique topography in that many of the areas under cultivation lie at 45° angles causing difficulties for cultivation, irrigation and harvesting. Its origins go back to 1765. French writer, Bernadin St Pierre, mentioned it in his novel *Paul and Virginie* in 1773. Nicholas Cere, the botanist, visited in 1782 and Matthew Flinders, the navigator and explorer, anchored at Baie du Cap in 1803 on his way back from Australia.

The factory was built around 1802 and was the first to install the horizontal cane crushing mill. The mill was introduced by the English planter, Charles Telfair, who acquired Bel Ombre in 1819. Originally cane was crushed by vertical cylinders rotated by oxen. Telfair transformed Bel Ombre into a 'model estate' by ensuring that the slaves were properly fed and housed.

In 1990 Bel Ombre hosted 'La Coupe de Canne', the official cane cutting ceremony, for the first time. The event, held each June, commemorates the opening of the season and takes place in one of the nineteen sugar estates. Representatives from each estate present a stick of sugar cane to the Minister of Agriculture for formal cutting by machette in a re-enactment of the days when it was cut by hand. This has mostly been replaced by machines. Field workers are given the day off to watch the ceremony which is attended by diplomats, politicians, sugar magnates, invited guests and the press. Such invitations are well worth taking up if visiting Mauritius in June.

North of Bel Ombre is the beautiful **Val Riche Forest**, which contains many fast disappearing indigenous trees. The area is owned by Bel Ombre and permission must be sought from the sugar estate office to enter. Winding steep tracks lead through veritable jungles of sugar cane from the B9 to **Frederica**. An old mill, a relic from the past, stands here on the site of an ancient sugar factory. Today edible palms are cultivated. The tracks climb and afford wonderful views of 2,000 acres (800 hectares) of indigenous forest.

At Val Riche there is a deer reserve with miradors or hunting platforms. Personnel from the Bel Ombre accompany visiting personages to the forest and entertain them at the Château of Bel Ombre, a grand colonial residence impeccably furnished with antiques of the French East India era and surrounded by lush gardens and lawns. The château is not open to the public.

A lovely 5km (3 mile) walk may be started from a wild, desolate and beautiful beach situated in front of the Bel Ombre factory eastwards to **Beau Champ** (Beautiful Field) where sugar cane fields almost tumble to the water's edge. Rejoin the main B9 road by cutting inland via narrow tracks bounded by sugar cane and thick plantations of wild banana trees where locals tend market gardens of chilli, beans and onions. Concealed amongst the cane fields are coral caves.

At Beau Champ, set back off the main road and concealed by a stately row of coconut palms is a large white bungalow surrounded by manicured gardens and lawns. A former hospital, it is now a private residence, occupied by employees of the sugar estate. Behind the complex heart of palm tree seedlings are matured in nurseries for planting out.

The coast road to Souillac continues past the bungalow and crosses the Beau Champ and Sainte Marie bridges over the River Jacotet. It cuts through jungly vegetation behind Beau Champ providing cool and peaceful areas for walks or picnics where *jacots* the Creole word for monkeys, perform antics along the tree-clad banks. The river flows out to the Bay Jacotet where at low tide it is possible to wade out to the isolated and uninhabited Îlot Sancho The islet was the scene of a violent attack by the British against the French just prior to their taking Mauritius in 1810. Some say it contains buried treasure on the island.

Small Hindu shrines with red pennants and Catholic shrines to Pere Laval are found near the iron bridge across the River des Galets. Just after the bridge a tiny roundabout indicates left for Chemin Grenier at 3km (2 miles) and straight on for Souillac.

The road follows a wild coast passing the small sugar factory of **Saint Felix**. A few kilometres ahead is the clean and safe beach of **Pointe aux Roches** with neatly trimmed lawns, picnic kiosks and observation platforms looking out to sea. On windy days fabulous views of surf beating against black rocks give the impression that the ocean is about to flood the land.

By a bus stop the Villas Pointe aux Roches, at a far safer location nearby, consists of twenty-six seafront bungalows. Three are equipped for self catering. Built in 1972 and under German/ Mauritian ownership, the well run hotel bar/restaurant has a comfortable and relaxing ambience with views of the beach to the east towards Riambel, an old Malagasy name meaning, 'the beach of sunshine.'

While swimming is safe from Pointe aux Roches, **Pomponnette**, a few kilometres eastwards with its inviting beach, has treacherous currents. There is a small complex of private bungalows near the scene of a tragic accident and skull and crossbone notices warn of the dangers of bathing. In 1969, a schoolteacher called Serge Alfred from Beau Bassin drowned while attempting to save the lives of four schoolgirls who had been swept out to sea. To recognise his bravery an impressive Olympic-size swimming pool complex was built at Beau Bassin and named after him.

At the SSR public beach near Surinam, Mauritians enjoy bathing and picnics on the filao fringed golden sands. Coastal paths afford invigorating walks to Pomponnette or to the village.

A lovely inland drive may be made to Bassin Blanc in the Savanne Mountains by taking the B10 from Chemin Grenier via Chamouny.
Few tourists venture this far and those that do are likely to be staying at Villas Pointe aux Roches. However, **Chemin Grenier** is a convenient stop for refreshments and provisions from its tumbledown shops and market. A bus terminal connects with Curepipe in the main street and there is a taxi stand where visitors can sit and watch the village go about its business without feeling intrusive. There is a post office, filling station, banks, bicycle repair shop and one or two bars where service is simple and friendly.

To get to Bassin Blanc take the B10 inland from the roundabout on the B9. At 3km (2 miles) there is a Y-junction. The B10 swings right for the detour to Chemin Grenier. The unmarked one-way street on the left leads to Chamouny where it links with the B89 to become a two-way road through sugar cane at the back of the village.

The B89 cuts straight through cane fields for 2km (1 mile) where the road splits into two. The right fork leads to Surinam but it is very easy to miss a small handwritten sign perched on a pole on the left indicating Mare Anguilles. Take this road which rises slowly for 3km (2 miles) through neglected tea plantations studded with patches of crimson wild raspberries. The plump fruits can be picked during the winter but are not as sweet as the cultivated variety.

Bassin Blanc is a water-filled crater at 500m (1,640ft) and from the summit there are impressive views of the Savanne Mountains

A shanty village of friendly locals at Chemin Grenier

Rochester Falls

The South Coast • 71

sweeping down to the coast. The crater is about 1km ($^1/_2$ mile) in circumference and is evidence of the island's volcanic origins. Over millions of years it filled with water and the banks are now clothed in dense vegetation. It is one of the last existing bird sanctuaries in native forest where access, is unrestricted. Visitors are asked to preserve its tranquil atmosphere and respect the birdlife. The surfaced road ends at Bassin Blanc where there are several Hindu shrines and thereafter degenerates into a rough walkable track through thick forestland northwards. The road leading to Bassin Blanc was constructed a few years ago to convey Hindu pilgrims to Grand Bassin further north for the annual Maha Shivaratree festival. (See Excursions from Curepipe section). Venturing beyond this point by car is really only suitable for four wheel drive vehicles.

Return to the B89 by retracing the route and turn left for Surinam passing the 1987 constructed **Mont Blanc Reservoir**. The white concrete building rises from the sugar cane fields like a monument to modern technology. **Surinam** is a large village with cyclone-scarred shops, churches and temples and concrete box-like dwellings cheerfully swathed in bright tropical vegetation. The road continues through the village where it links again with the B9 coast road to Souillac. An old iron bridge crosses the River Patate before sweeping round the bay and into town.

Souillac is the main south coast town. The narrow inlets allow fishing boats to find sanctuary where the Patate and Savanne rivers form an estuary. The Savanne Mountains form a dramatic backdrop. The town was named after the French governor Vicomte François de Souillac who enhanced the social life of the island during his years of governorship between 1779 and 1787. Prior to the era of road and rail, sugar was taken by overnight steamer from Souillac to Port Louis, a procedure that involved days. Remnants of the old port can still be seen and radical changes are being made to convert the area around the old port of Souillac westwards to Riambel into a touristic site improving facilities for locals and to encourage visitors.

Taxis from Souillac make the bone jerking return journey through sugar cane fields to **Rochester Falls**. The more adventurous can drive or walk the 5km (3 miles) by following the signs for Rochester Falls along the Lady Barclay Branch Road to the left of the large Roman Catholic Church in the main road. Signs marked 'Rochester Hall' in conflicting directions confuse the most determined explorer who should simply keep right, past La Terracine sugar factory and a colourful Indian temple. The rough track, weaves uphill between the cane fields before descending to the falls. They tumble from the Savanne River from a height of about 10m (33ft) where constant

72 • Visitor's Guide: Mauritius, Rodrigues & Reunion

erosion has fashioned the basalt rock into upright columns. Young Indian boys squat at the top waiting for tourists to arrive and perform dare-devil dives into the water below.

In Souillac the tranquil **Telfair Gardens** (named after Charles Telfair of Bel Ombre), across the road from the post office, are worth visiting and are permanently open. There are public toilets, picnic areas and a kiosk. Gigantic Indian almond trees and banyans provide shade over trimmed lawns and wooden benches overlooks the sea. Steps lead down to a small beach where youngsters swim in spite of the skull and crossbone warning signs. There are poignant views of Souillac Cemetery across the bay to the west. The cemetery contains many nineteenth-century tombs, including those of Mauritian poet, Robert Edward Hart and the historian Baron d'Unienville. Graves of Muslims, Hindus and Christians have been destroyed by savage sea and cyclone damage. Plans exist to construct a sea wall to prevent further erosion and to renovate the paths and tombstones.

Turn right outside the gardens where a road, bordered by bungalows with shaded courtyards, leads to the former house of Robert Edward Hart (1891-1954). Hart was the librarian of the Mauritius Institute and in 1935 became the first president of the Society of Mauritian Writers. His writings characterised the sounds, smells and colours of Mauritius and he sought inspiration from the beauty of natural surroundings. The old coral-built bungalow with polished red floors is now a museum containing books, manuscripts personal belongings and a visitor's book. Doors open to a patio at the back giving breathtaking views of a golden beach where ferocious seas have pounded smooth the black basalt rocks. His portrait bears an uncanny resemblance to a silhouetted black and white photograph of La Roche qui Pleure (an outcrop of rocks further up the coast).

Le Gris Gris, a 10-minute stroll from the museum, is reputed to be linked with black magic. There are no sorcerers today, but the atmosphere lingers. It is the island's most southerly point and is more like the windswept coasts of the Scottish highlands than the gentle shores of a tropical island. A shelter overlooks a wide yellow beach where weather-bent filao trees attest to the ferocity of the wind.

The Gris Gris Guest House nearby has three simple double rooms for rent. Snacks and drinks are taken in a pleasant restaurant and Creole and European meals are cooked to order.

Beyond Le Gris Gris, a surfaced road bordered by sugar cane on the left and sea on the right, leads to the Foyer of Notre Dame de L'Unite, a religious weekend retreat run by Catholic nuns. Notices at the entrance warn that it is private property but there is a belfry further on giving access to the chapel for private prayer.

Magnificent coastal walks can be enjoyed by continuing past the chapel for about 100yd where a thin chain fences off undulating heathland belonging to the Saint Aubin Sugar Estate. Locals ignore the signs and nobody will mind as long as respect is shown for the land. Lovely walks give access to a coast black basalt cliffs with rocky headlands, amongst them La Roche qui Pleure, so named because as the sea cascades around it, it seems to be weeping.

From Souillac the A9 turns northwards to Curepipe crossing the River des Negresses via the tree-lined avenues of St Aubin Sugar Estate. Isolated Indian temples sprout from cane fields before the road bridges the Rivière des Anguilles. From the bridge there are spectacular views of luxuriant vegetation and forests of straggly travellers trees adorning the banks of the boulder strewn river.

To continue the south coast tour, turn right just after the bridge on to the B8 for the large village of **Rivière des Anguilles** where **La Vanille Crocodile Park** at 2km (1 mile) is well signposted. It was opened in 1985 and occupies the valley of a former vanilla growing area. The site is the equivalent of a tropical rain forest with exotic palms, freshwater streams and local flora and fauna.

The park is the brainchild of Owen Griffiths, an Australian zoologist and his Mauritian wife who discovered that the area was suitable for the farming of Nile crocodiles. The first crocodiles, one male and four females, were imported from Madagascar and their offspring placed in heated indoor nurseries for one year before they were released into ponds.

The crocodiles are kept in secure enclosures, according to age, until they reach maturity. The site is a tourist attraction with a collection of monkey, deer, giant tortoise, tenrec, rabbits, bats, wild pig and a giant Telfair Skink which is indigenous to Round Island. There is also an exhibition room containing specimens of Mascarene reptiles with descriptive notes in English. Among the exhibits are the luminous green True Chameleon and one of the largest species of lizard, the Giant phelsuma from Madagascar. There is a car park, restaurant/snack bar and toilets. Mosquitoes are particularly rampant. Repellant is on sale at the entrance.

A detour may be made to **Tyack**, a few kilometres from Rivière des Anguilles village on the A9 Curepipe-Souillac road to the former house and Museum of Sookdeo Bissoondoyal. Born in 1908, Bissoondoyal turned from school teaching to politics in 1948 and remained a Member of the Legislative Assembly until 7 years before his death in 1977. Deeply revered by the Indian community he formed a political party called the Independent Forward Block in

Creole woman holding **bredes** *or edible greens*

The True Chameleon from Madagascar

1957. The small white and green Creole house in which he was born contains his personal belongings and books.

If continuing north on the A9 to Curepipe it is worth stopping to admire the magnificent gardens of the Britannia Sugar Estate which lie to the north of Tyack. It is the only estate owned by a foreign company (the British Lonhro Group). Visits to the factory and grounds can be arranged on request with the Public Relations Officer (see the Additional Information section at the end of this chapter).

The A9 heads north to the tea growing highlands of Bois Cheri and Nouvelle France where the motorway links Plaisance Airport with the north. From here there is easy access to Curepipe or Mahebourg.

Alternatively a more picturesque route is to take the B8 from Rivière des Anguilles to Plaine Magnien through villages and the sugar estates of Savannah and Mon Tresor-Mon Desert. The road crosses mid-nineteenth century bridges, over the Dragon, St Amand and Du Poste rivers which flow from the Mare aux Vacoas area in the central uplands. The little bridge crossing the River St Amand collapsed in June 1878 and was hastily re-erected 2 months later. Finally it was safely reconstructed by the Public Works Department in 1936. Travellers palms grow in profusion around the river.

A permit can be obtained from the police station at L 'Escalier to visit **Le Souffleur** on the coast. A short drive leads to the beach where Le Souffleur or a 'blowhole' is fashioned in a dramatic outcrop of rock. Thirty years ago Mauritians were delighted by the ferocity of the water jet that shot skywards when the seas were rough. Unfortunately constant erosion has enlarged the blowhole and today the jet is little more than a cloud of spray. Care should be taken when scrambling over the rocks.

Just beyond L'Escalier the road opens out to explore an avenue of bottle palms on the right leading to the administrative offices of the Savannah Sugar Estate. The large isolated building, surrounded by pristine plots of tropical flowers, is perched at the top of a hill with views of sugar cane fields sweeping down to the south-east coast.

Plaine Magnien is a bustling village with all the amenities of a small town. The Tourist Rendezvous Hotel, in the centre, provides accommodation for businessmen and the odd tourist as it is close to the airport. From Plaine Magnien the A10 runs direct to Curepipe via the strung out village of Rose Belle.

The airport occupies the area of **Plaisance**. Known simply as Plaisance Airport by tongue-tied tourists and foreign airline pilots, it took its present name, Sir Seewoosagur Ramgoolam International Airport (after the former Prime Minister) in December 1987 when a new terminal was built.

An incredible discovery was made in the marshlands just south of the airport in 1865. George Weldon, a British schoolteacher and amateur naturalist, had a keen interest in finding the remains of the extinct dodo. When he heard that a French sugar planter was excavating the marshlands for fertilizer he made a deeper search. His enthusiasm was rewarded when he unearthed an almost intact set of bones which he was convinced belonged to the dodo. They were dispatched to England and verified by experts who assembled them into a complete skeleton. Later excavations by Clark and a Mauritian naturalist, Theodore Sauzier, resulted in the reconstruction of the dodo that is in the Port Louis Museum.

A good road south-east from the airport leads through sugar cane fields for $7^1/_2$ km (5 miles) to Beachcomber's latest resort complex, the luxurious 185 roomed Shandrani Hotel at Le Chaland. The hotel is situated on a private peninsular with three separate beaches. All rooms have sea view and guests are offered tennis, squash, volleyball, windsurfing, waterskiing and water sports facilities. All these activities are free except scuba diving. There is a gymnasium, sauna, conference facilities and a full entertainments and excursion programme.

Additional Information

Britannia Sugar Estate
Contact the Public Relations Officer
☎ 626 2532

Rivière des Anguilles
La Vanille Crocodile Park
Open: daily from 9.30am-5pm.
☎ 626 2503

Souillac
Robert Edward Hart Museum
Open: daily 9am-4pm except
Tuesdays, Fridays and public
holidays.
Admission free.

Tyack
Sookdeo Bissoondoyal Museum
Open: daily 9am-4pm except
Tuesdays, Fridays and public
holidays.

Tourist information and car hire is
available from:

Chemin Grenier
Villas Pointe aux Roches Hotel
☎ 626 2507

SSR (Plaisance) Airport
*Mauritius Government Tourist Office
    Information Counter*
☎ 637 3635
Open: depending on flight
arrivals/departures.
Also car hire and tour operator
desks.

Shandrani Hotel
$7^1/_2$ km (5 miles) from SSR Airport
☎ 631 9511

4
THE WEST COAST

The west coast, from the south of Port Louis to Le Morne Peninsula, stretches for a distance of about 48km (30 miles). The A3 from the capital meanders inland along a well surfaced road with constant and worthwhile access to the sea on the one hand and mountains on the other, before hugging the coast from Tamarin to Black River where it becomes the B9. From here the B9 continues southwards for another 20km (12 miles) to Baie du Cap.

The whole coast is dominated by mountains. After leaving Port Louis the angles of Corps de Garde, Rempart, Trois Mamelles and in the distance to the south-west, as if a separate island, the solid mound-shaped Le Morne Brabant, provide a unique spectacle of familiar landmarks from a fresh perspective. A profusion of mountains and forest of the Black River area and the beaches of Flic en Flac and Le Morne appeal to both wildlife and water sports enthusiasts.

Just after Pointe aux Sables the coastline loses its protective reef allowing Indian Ocean breakers to pound basalt cliffs. Albion has a calm bay and is adjacent to bracing cliff walks. From Flic en Flac southwards the coral reef re-appears as far as Le Morne Peninsula endowing it with the familiar blue lagoons.

The west is renowned for its lack of rainfall yet sugar cane grows in profusion. Overhead irrigation equipment resembling steel robots with outstretched arms spray fierce jets of water over ribbons of cane fields. When driving, these dry roads may be slippery. The land lies in the administrative district of Black River bounded by Port Louis to the north, the central plateau towns to the east and the Savanne Mountains to the south. Medine and Bel Ombre Sugar Estates own most of the land under cane cultivation.

Pointe aux Sables is really an extension of Port Louis. Take the Route Royale out of the capital and just after crossing the Grand

78 • Visitor's Guide: Mauritius, Rodrigues & Reunion

River North West, Pointe aux Sables is signposted on the right along the B31. The Vagrant Depot, a grey stone legacy of British colonialism built in 1865, is a national monument. It is situated on the left hand side at 100m (328ft) just before the road rises and swings to the right for Pointe aux Sables.

It is an uninspiring village with a few stores and cheap hotels and basic beach bungalows for rent. Next door to the Villa Lys d'Or Bungalows the public beach consists of a strip of sand backed by a picnic area shaded by filao trees and views across to the industrial installations of Port Louis harbour. Beyond the village on an isolated scrubby headland is the oddly attractive, Le Petit Verger Prison with its high walls bathed in barbed wire and bougainvillea. The B31 turns inland and degenerates into a rough pot-holed track to **Petite Rivière** on the A3 main road. Here women use the gulleys of fast running water from the Grand River North West as an outdoor launderette.

Detour to the west coast by turning right on to the B78 from Petite Rivière and right again at 2km (1 mile) to reach the lighthouse at **Pointe aux Caves.** The road passes the Belle Vue Rice Experimental Station on the side where rice is grown experimentally under the auspices of the Ministry of Agriculture. At a T-junction a little way

Flic en Flac on the west coast

along take the left fork for the lighthouse.

Built in 1904, the lighthouse stands at 30m (100ft). It has seventy-seven steps and is the only fully automated lighthouse in working order on the mainland. From the top there are outstanding views of the mountain ranges of Port Louis and the coast towards Flic en Flac. The keeper, who lives in a bungalow nearby may give a guided tour depending on his mood. The lighthouse is perched on black craggy rock where caves used to contain colonies of swallows. Sadly the population has declined due to vandalism and the local taste for bird's nest soup. Some believe that the caves form an underground link with Reunion but this has never been proved. They are deep and exploration should only be undertaken with an experienced guide. North of the lighthouse are some pathways giving access to walks along high grassy topped cliffs.

On the B78 is **Albion,** a desirable residential area where modern private seaside bungalows overlook a tranquil sandy bay. It is possible to drive directly onto the beach along a hard sandy track. To the east the Corp de Garde stands over the peaks of the Petit and Grand Malabar mountains while to the north there are views of the lighthouse at Pointe aux Caves. The beach is long, white and deserted and swimming is safe within the coral reef.

At the A3 turn right for Flic en Flac where the road meanders south bissecting a wide and fertile plain separating the plateau towns from a delectable coast of low cliffs. Here the busy village of **Bambous** with its wide flamboyant tree-shaded avenues and pretty dwellings boast all the attributes of a small town complete with police station, fuel station, post office, banks and shops. Its large basalt built Roman Catholic Church with the large white cross of Jesus Christ in the well tended lawns is worth inspection. To the right of the church is a large rockery surrounded by blue iron railings containing thanksgiving notes and flowers. The main road veers right through the village and towards the entrance of the Medine Sugar Estate.

Two kilometres (1 mile) after the Medine Sugar Estate entrance turn right for **Flic en Flac**. The road is signposted, well surfaced and descends gently through sugar cane fields to the coast. The resort has developed quickly and its proximity to Port Louis and the plateau towns have made it an ideal residential area for locals.

At the northern end of the beach Villas Caroline with its individual chalets is ideal for self-caterers. The rooms overlook an enormous white sand beach complete with shallow lagoon. There is a diving school attached to the hotel where diving equipment can be hired and information provided on various diving sites.

The coral reefs in this area are of particular interest to marine

The West Coast • 81

conservationists and divers. The Mauritius Marine Conservation Group were concerned at the lack of marine life around the reef and in 1983 efforts to create an artificial reef by sinking a barge met with only a slight increase in marine life. Since then successful reefs have been constructed in other areas by using similar methods.

There used to be mud flats behind the beach at Flic en Flac and folklore maintains that the name comes from the sound of boots squelching through the mud. The public beach can get crowded at weekends but at other times it is a paradise of soft white sand fringed with filao trees and gentle views of Le Morne in the south.

The regular bus service to Flic en Flac from Rose Hill and Quatre Bornes takes about 45 minutes with townbound services terminating at around 5pm. At the end of the day great groups of families and friends form orderly colourful queues and wait patiently for the homebound bus. Queue-jumpers incur the disapproval of the waiting crowd. On the beach there are public toilets, a couple of snack stalls and several Chinese restaurants offering value for money seafood and local dishes in an unpretentious atmosphere. Most stay open till around 10pm.

There is a good standard of smaller hotels, guesthouses and private bungalows with small stores for the self-caterer. The Manissa Hotel opposite the public beach by the bus stop has a comfortable restaurant with delicious Indian specialities.

Flic en Flac caters for all visitors and is a wonderful place to wander and sample the cosmopolitan island atmosphere. Yet in spite of its recent development, like many resorts, it sleeps at night, save for entertainment in the hotels. Villas Caroline organise a nightly programme of music and dancing and theme evenings for guests and non-guests at reasonable prices. La Pirogue, at Wolmar, is the largest hotel on the west coast with prices geared to the international market. Visitors seeking a night out pay an entrance fee, half of which is refundable in the form of gaming chips to ensure a visit to the casino. The hotel is renowned for its excellent service and full range of sports and activities. Beyond La Pirogue is the luxurious Imperial Garden Sofitel Hotel.

Return to the A3 and turn right to continue southwards to Tamarin. At 1km ($^1/_2$ mile) on the left an avenue of coconut palms heralds the approach to **Casela Bird Park**. Here a well surfaced road leads past bushes of bougainvillea and the stillest of ponds which mirrors the reflections of Rempart Mountain behind it.

Casela is home to 142 species of birds including the lovely long necked Pink Pigeons which until recently were threatened with extinction. The lovely dusky pink birds were donated by the Black

River Aviary and can be seen alongside hundreds of other exotics from Asia, Australasia, Africa and the Americas. A guide to the park is available at the entrance.

The park covers 25 acres (10 hectares) and sits on the flanks of Rempart Mountain with views of cane clothed countryside rolling down to the west coast. There is a restaurant and snack bar and walks criss-crossing ponds and streams. Down a set of steps beyond the aviaries there is a mini-zoo of tigers, monkeys, lemurs, stag and a lake of graceful flamingos.

Leaving Casela on the A3 there are lovely mountain vistas. Le Morne appears to rise over Tamarin while inland in the distance lie the Black River mountains and the bulk of Rempart. After crossing the 1964-built Rempart Bridge there is a small roundabout.

The first exit leads along rough sugar cane tracks to Tamarin Estate, the deer estate of Yemen, and the Magenta Dam and power-house in the foothills of the Vacoas Mountains. The road to the Magenta Dam is on private land and permission to enter should be sought from the Central Water Authority. The road winds through thick forests of eucalyptus trees and runs level with a pipeline to the power house and thereafter rises very steeply along a concrete pathway up the flanks of the Vacaos Mountains and Tamarin Falls. An easier route to Tamarin Falls is described under the 'Excursions from Curepipe' section in Chapter 6.

Back on the A3 the second exit from the roundabout leads to Tamarin along a good well made road bordered by deep pink and white oleander bushes. **Tamarin** is named after the tamarind trees that were introduced by the Dutch. These trees grow profusely along the west coast. Just before reaching the village the road swings sharply left where there is a speed limit warning sign of 65kph (40mph). This is followed by another sharp right hand bend on the 1934 iron built Tamarin Bridge over the wide Tamarin river.

The village lies in a tranquil bay at the mouth of the River du Rempart and River Tamarin and seems to have stood still despite tourism development.

Access to the public beach is just after the attractive Roman Catholic church and school of St Benoit. Private bungalows nearby are available for rent. The beach is totally unspoilt with views of Tamarin Mountain rising to 548m (1,797ft) in the distance. Here the coral reef is subdued by fresh water from the rivers flowing down from the central highlands. When the winds are in the right direction waves break onto a glorious beach although locals complain that the ferocity of waves has declined in recent years. The clean beach has toilets and pavillions. Locals fish upstream where the fertile river banks are lined with scarlet blossomed nourouk trees.

Tamarin is famous for its salt. Before salt processing was established in Mauritius it had to be imported from Madagascar. The salt is extracted by solar evaporation and piled into great rectangular pans. Fishing is the mainstay of Tamarin community and a Fishermen Co-operative Centre of 'Maison des Pecheurs' with cold storage facilities is located off Market Street. Here fresh fish is sold direct to the public at reasonable prices. The Cheshire Home Workshop a yellow and white low slung Creole building in the main road, displays and sells local handicrafts.

The A3 continues to the Black River (Rivière Noire) area. The estuary of the Grand Rivière Noire (Big Black River) is the outlet of a waterway which has tumbled through some of the most rugged areas of Mauritius. Inland the steep sided splendour of the Black River Gorges with its nooks and crannies provided perfect shelter for the *marrons* or runaway slaves of the nineteenth century. The gorges make great walking country and are described in the 'Excursions from Curepipe' section in Chapter 6. The Black River area has no towns, only sparsley populated villages and hamlets, where Afro-Creole performs impromptu performances of the *sega*.

Rempart Mountain

84 • Visitor's Guide: Mauritius, Rodrigues & Reunion

The Black River area has a special appeal in spite of its isolation. To the north the picturesque hamlet of **La Mivoie** has its share of the tourism market with the Shellorama Shell Museum and La Ravanne, where souvenirs may be bought and a delightful restaurant specialising in seafood and French cuisine called La Bonne Chute near the forecourt of the Caltex fuel station.

Less than 1km ($^1/_2$ mile) after La Mivoie is **La Preneuse** hamlet named after a French warship that was chased by a British squadron during the Napoleonic Wars. La Preneuse took refuge in the Black River where a shore battery was set up. Here the clean and simple Les Bougainvillea Auberge provides simple rooms overlooking a white beach and the passing visitor may take refreshments on the lawn Beyond the auberge is the Martello Tower and public beach and to get there take the right turn off the A3 which is signposted Les Bougainvilleas. This is a small coast road which eventually links with the main A3 near Rivière Noire.

Continue along the A3 to the village of **Grand Rivière Noire** where a sign on the right indicates the Black River Post Office and Cemetery. Friendly post office staff or any locals will help locate the tomb of Colonel Edward Draper, an English Army officer, whose passion for horse-racing, led to the founding of the Mauritius Turf Club at Champs de Mars in 1812.

The Black River area is renowned for big game fishing. Between September and March marlin, sailfish, wahoo, yellow fin tuna, and various species of shark migrate to the warm waters around Mauritius and feed just beyond the reef where the sea bed falls abruptly to a depth of 600m (1,968ft). At Centre de Peche, the Rivière Noire centre specialises in big game fishing. The sport is an important tourist attraction and provides for the development of the local smoked fish industry. After excited participants pose for photographs the catch is taken to local smoke-houses to be processed as smoked marlin and sold to restaurants and hotels. The appearance of this delicacy is not unlike smoked salmon although the flavour is slightly richer and saltier.

At the south end of the village at the National Community Health Development Centre a signpost indicates a road to the right where there is a tourist area containing the Rivière Noire Hotel, the Hotel Club and the Magnum 44 Disco. Both hotels have information on big game fishing excursions. Near the police station are the Black River Aviaries where efforts are being made to save threatened birds from extinction. Entry is restricted to ornithologists and scientists although Mauritours sometimes arrange group tours.

A good place for lunch is the Jade Pavillion Restaurant lying in the

The West Coast • 85

foothills of Tamarin Mountain on the A3 to Le Morne. Opposite the restaurant a walkable track leads to the Yemen Deer Estate at 3km (2 miles) and the Black River gorges. Shortly afterwards the A3 crosses the 1928 built Rivière Noire Bridge and ascends gently with views of Le Morne and Benitiers Island to the south. More salt pans and another Martello Tower lie on the coast side of the peninsular known as Les Salines but access is restricted at weekends.

From here the A3 changes its identity to become the B9 and continues to the estuary of the muddy Petite Rivière Noire (Little Black River). Its beauty lies inland for the mountains which spawn this stream are a continuation of those which form the Black River Gorge. This area is so extensive in its ruggedness as to be without doubt the most dramatic and beautiful of the island's interior. Southwards from Petite Rivière Noire the road hugs a rocky shore for a distance of 4km (2 miles) where the sparse hamlets of Petite and Grande Case Noyale are the only signs of life.

At **Petite Case Noyale** opposite the administrative buildings of the Civil Status Office, dispensary and post office, is a private deer reserve belonging to Bel Ombre Sugar Estate. The farm was started in 1976 with thirty-four deer captured from the forests. In 1980 the Company Deer Farming was created and with careful breeding there are now over 1,200 animals which provide venison for local consumption. Coffee grown on the slopes of Chamarel is processed in a small factory inside the reserve.

It is worth making a detour from **Grande Case Noyale**, via Chamarel, to Baie du Cap. From here the B9 returns via Le Morne peninsular passing through sugar cane fields and unspoilt villages.

'Case' means house in Creole and the area of Grand Case Noyale was named after a retired French soldier called Noyale who ran a small guesthouse for travellers in the eighteenth century. He was eventually murdered by runaway slaves.

The 1939 built white corrugated roofed church of Mater Dolorosa at Grande Case Noyale lies at the foot of a steep winding road. Here a sign indicates Chamarel inland at 5km (3 miles). In 1812 a rough road was cut to access the remote Chamarel area but is now well surfaced. It climbs steeply into the timbered foothills of the Black River Mountains until a Y-junction indicates left for Les Marres and Plaine Champagne on the central plateau and right for the village of Chamarel. The area of Chamarel is, a fertile plateau where coffee is grown on slopes of lovely wooded country. It was named after Antoine de Chamarel, a former French Army Captain and land-owner who farmed vanilla, coffee and pepper. At **La Crete** just before reaching Chamarel village, there are panoramic views of Le Morne,

Île aux Benitiers and the islet Malaise set within the turquoise lagoon.

Chamarel village, with its church, village hall and cyclone-proof houses is remarkably undeveloped in spite of the number of visitors passing through to visit the Cascade Chamarel and the Coloured Earths. Although popular with tourists efforts to keep the area natural and remote have been successful.

The Coloured Earths of Chamarel were promoted as Mauritius' first tourist attraction way back in the 1960s. Even today souvenir test-tubes containing the multi-coloured earth can be bought from beachvendors and tourist boutiques. Specimens of the earth can also be bought from the little yellow-roofed administration building at the entrance of the site. The land belongs to Bel Ombre Sugar Estate and a small entrance charge is made to visit the earths. An example of the horizontal mill, like a giants washing mangle, lies in front of the administration building. It was introduced by Charles Telfair, one of Bel Ombre's first owners.

Sunrise is the best time to see the Coloured Earths. At other times coaches and hire cars full of tourists wend their way along tortuous potholed tracks bounded by sugar cane to find no refreshment and a rather disappointing sight. However geologists are still intrigued by the rolling dunes of multi-coloured lunar-like landscape. The colours, red, brown, violet, green, blue, purple and yellow never erode in spite of torrential downpours and adverse climatic conditions. The phenomena has never been explained but it is believed the earths are composed of mineral rich volcanic ash.

Of more stunning beauty are the 83m (272ft) high Cascade Chamarel. They fall from the River St Denis in the Black River Mountains and plunge seaward to form the River du Cap. Wooden walkways from the roadway enable closer views of the waterfalls.

To leave the area of the Coloured Earths re-trace the route to the administrative building at the entrance. Turn left to return to Chamarel village and Plaine Champagne but as most people combine a shopping trip to Curepipe with Plaine Champagne this itinerary is described in the 'Excursions from Curepipe' section.

Turn right in front of the administration building for Baie du Cap via Choisy in the south. The road descends gently through sugar cane fields and thick plantations of banana trees and travellers palms. As a reminder that this is a tortuous route, ramshackle buses operating between Chamarel and Baie du Cap may suddenly appear on one of the hairpin bends. In spite of obvious dangers from other road users, the drive should be slow and sedate to really experience the lush tumbling views of vegetation. It is particularly striking during June when great feathery flowers sprout from the ripened

Workers at the Tamarin salt pans

The giant tortoise, one of the unusual animals to be found on Mauritius

sugar cane like colossal clouds of candifloss.

At Baie du Cap village turn right to rejoin the B9 to Le Morne. Here the road hugs the shoreline of the Macconde headlands before sweeping deep into Baie du Cap lying at the foot of the steep Savanne Mountains. Access across the bay is via a raised cement platform, colloquially termed in the local plans as 'the Irishman's Bridge'. In January and February heavy rains tumbling down the mountain slopes and into the Baie du Cap River cause the area to flood turning the blue waters into a deep reddish brown colour.

La Prairie Public Beach, with trimmed lawns and profusion of filaos, lies just beyond Baie du Cap with views of Îlot Fourneau. The next village, **Le Morne**, with its widespread shanty dwellings and Afro-Creole inhabitants, is typical of the Black River area. Just after the end of the village at the community centre the road penetrates thick woodland and rises gently before descending in a series of sharp bends towards Le Morne Peninsula. In summer the area is ablaze with the crimson red flamboyant trees.

A road to the left of the B9 leads to **Le Morne Peninsula**. It is the most westerly point of Mauritius and juts out like a hammer head. At the centre is the 555m (1,820ft) high table-topped mountain called Le Morne Brabant. Runaway slaves used the mountain as a retreat hiding among the precipitous flanks and chasms to evade capture by search parties. When slavery was abolished in 1835 a posse was sent to Le Morne to announce the news. The slaves believed that they were to be hunted down and rather than submit to arrest, flung themselves from the summit to their deaths.

The peninsula is dominated by Beachcomber's Le Paradis-Brabant Hotel complex which claims to be the biggest resort property in the Indian Ocean. It is really two hotels in one, Le Paradis and Le Brabant. Beyond them beautiful beaches, backed by idyllic woodland and forest walks, hug the entire peninsular and an unbroken reef protects a perfectly calm lagoon. The hotels are within walking distance of each other and share the same entertainment programme and facilities. The Paradis is more geared to families and offers a babysitting service and mini club for youngsters while the Brabant, livelier and larger of the two, includes a casino, gymnasium, 9-hole golf course, a full range of water sports including deep sea fishing, tennis and football. They are the only hotels in Mauritius which offer horse-riding facilities.

A security guard at the entrance keeps undesirables out. Guests staying at other Beachcomber hotels are issued with a Beachcomber Card which entitles them to use the facilities of other hotels in the group. Non-guests are charged an entrance fee. The nearest bus stop is 4km (2 miles) away on the B9.

The hotels have excellent restaurants catering for all tastes. However the Domino Seafood Restaurant, 1km ($^1/_2$ mile) away, offers an unusual alternative. Set on the slopes of Le Morne Brabant, it serves seafood lunches and Chinese specialities on outdoor terraces giving magnificent panoramas of Île aux Benitiers and a delightful deer reserve. The restaurant is well indicated from the hotels. Continue up the track where a small car park is situated beneath the restaurant.

The land and Le Morne mountain are privately owned by the Gambier family. Permission to climb on or around the mountain should be sought from them. Enquiries may be made to the manager of the restaurant or the hotel. Guides are available to conduct safaris into the deer reserve.

Midway along the B9 at 6km (4 miles) between Grand Case Noyale and Le Morne Peninsula is the attractive village of **La Gaulette**. Tropical flowers and shrubs grow in profusion in neat front gardens and it is worth stopping here to watch the world go by from the spacious verandah of the pagoda style café/restaurant of Cafe La Gaulette. Across the road the Shell Museum, sells jade jewellery, coral, shells and local handicrafts. At the end of the village is a small Indian temple. The road bounded by sugar cane fields retraces the northward route back to Port Louis.

Additional Information

Black River (area)
Shellorama Shell Museum
Open: Monday to Friday, 9.30am-4pm
☎ 683 6704
There is also a branch at La Gaulette.

Black River Government Aviary
Not open to the public but visits may be possible through Mauritours at Rose Hill on ☎ 454 3078 or through their representatives at most hotels.

Chamarel
Chamarel Coloured Earths
Open: every day, excluding public holidays. No toilets or refreshments. As there is no road lighting visitors should leave the area by 4pm. Admission fee.

Flic en Flac
Casela Bird Park
☎ 208 5041 or 212 6001
Open: every day including public holidays. October to March, 9am-6pm, April to September 9am-5pm. Admission fee.

Permission to visit Magenta Dam area should be obtained from:
Central Water Authority
Head Office
Port Louis
☎ 212 5129

Tourist information and car hire is available from all hotels and travel agents.

5

PORT LOUIS

Port Louis is the capital and commercial centre of Mauritius. It lies in a sheltered harbour in the north-west surrounded by an amphitheatre of mountains known as the Moka Range. Its distinctive peaks, knolls and mounds provide a picturesque landscape which have always fascinated and inspired those who come here.

From the sea, looking from right to left, the bulk of Signal Mountain at 328m (1,076ft) dominates the city. Next, Le Pouce (The Thumb) at 811m (2,660ft) rises from the south wing of the Moka Range in a thumbs up sign. The most distinctive peak of all, at 818m (2,683ft), comes in the form of Pieter Both whose pinnacle in the shape of a round head appears perched precariously on what looks like the cloak shrouded shoulders of a man. It is said that the day Pieter Both loses its head some great catastrophe will destroy the island but in truth the head is so well fixed that it would take an earthquake to move it. Closer to the city to the north is a knoll known as La Citadelle or Fort Adelaide with the crumbling remains of a fortress at its crest. At 83m (272ft) it is not too much to walk and from the summit the views of Port Louis and the harbour are rewarding.

Port Louis began as a primitive harbour. In 1722 the infant French East India Company transferred their headquarters from the old Dutch settlement at Warwyck Bay (now Mahebourg) to what was then North West Harbour. It was renamed Port Louis after Louis XV of France although some historians believe it was named after Port Louis in Brittany from where many French seamen set sail for India.

In 1735 Bertrand François Mahé de Labourdonnais arrived as the newly appointed Governor-General of the Mascarene Islands and finding Port Louis in an utter shambles went about transforming it into a thriving sea port and commercial centre. He is the acknowledged founder of Port Louis and his statue at Place d'Armes over-

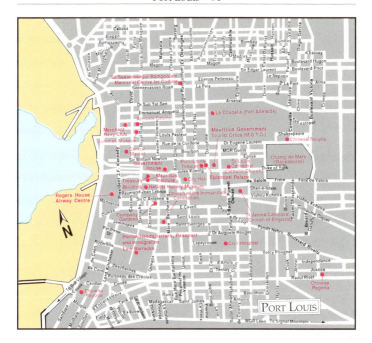

looking the harbour is one of the most famous landmarks of the city.

Under British rule Port Louis developed into a major port. Its excellent harbour facilities had been constructed with the sailing ship in mind, but by the end of the nineteenth century with the introduction of the steamer and the opening of the Suez Canal Port Louis declined in importance as a major shipping centre. Outbreaks of disease, cyclone and fire caused many of its inhabitants to flee to the plateau towns.

Port Louis was originally confined to the flatlands between La Citadelle and Signal Mountain but today spreads in neat blocks to the foothills of the Moka Range. Banks, government buildings, offices and shops attest to its importance as the thriving commercial centre of the island.

The harbour has come a long way since the days of sail and its activities have undoubtedly increased. It is essentially a working harbour and the quays are not really equipped to receive cruise ships although they have been known to call. Administered by the Mauritius Marine Authority the harbour provides cargo handling services and facilities for containerised and conventional traffic. The Bulk Sugar Terminal constructed in July 1980 allows sugar to be loaded at the rate of 1,400 tons per hour along with storage facilities. The government have also approved a port development plan which will enable it to cater for increased shipping up to the year 2000.

There are two bus stations: Immigration Square Bus Station just off the dual carriageway near the harbour serves the north. Buses to the south via Curepipe operate from Victoria Square to the west of the city close to Line Barracks. Both have taxi ranks and public toilets although avoid using the ones located at Victoria Square unless in cases of dire emergency. Timetables are available but are rarely necessary as buses leave every few minutes during working hours.

The best way to see Port Louis is on foot. A street map of the city is available from the Mauritius Government Tourist Office but visitors should note that some streets have been renamed. Even Mauritians find it confusing and many prefer to stick to the former French names. For instance, Desforges Street is also known as Sir Seewoosagur Ramgoolam Street, Place d'Armes as Place Sookdeo Bissondoyal, Gillet Square as Nelson Mandela Square and so on. All streets are clearly marked with nameplates.

Throughout the day it is often hot, humid and boisterous. Modern air conditioned offices stand beside cyclone battered buildings, some over a hundred years old. Their overhanging verandahs provide instant cover from sudden downpours of tropical rain, which when it comes, provoke a sign of relief from city workers ruffled by the heat. Food vendors chorus *dholl puri* (a pancake topped with fiery red chilli sauce) and *gateaux piments* (fried chilli cakes) to passers by and small traders spread their wares across narrow pavements.

During the day Port Louis swirls with people, most of whom live in the cooler plateau towns in the south and commute by public transport or car. After 5pm there is a mass exodus of its working population and most restaurants and shops close. The city operates a one-way system and parking, apart from in Place d'Armes which is reserved for taxis, is unrestricted and untidy. Pavements dating back to Labourdonnais' time are in poor repair, so the wearing of comfortable flat shoes is recommended. In the city centre deep gulleys between the pavement and road collect the heavy rainfalls of December to April. Care is needed when crossing the road although most drivers will stop at pedestrian crossings.

Strolling round Port Louis on a Saturday afternoon or Sunday affords the opportunity of viewing some of its lovelier sights without the hustle and bustle of a weekday. The city is a curious mix of the seedy and the sophisticated with few places to sit and watch it go by.

In spite of this it is rich in history and there are pockets of picturesque parks, delightful Creole houses and some excellent restaurants. Many statues, declared National Monuments, around the city centre symbolise the island's colonial ties with France and Britain.

The heart of the city is **Place d'Armes** (Place Sookdeo Bissoondoyal) where the statue of Labourdonnais looks out across the harbour. Behind it is a Fleur de Lys monument commemorating the 250th anniversary of the founding of Port Louis in 1735 and three busts of modern day Mauritian politicians, namely Doctor Maurice Curé, the founder of the Labour Party, Renganden Seeneevasen (1910-58) and Emmanuel Anquetil (1885-1946).

Behind Place d'Armes two palm tree-lined avenues, Duke of Edinburgh on the left and Queen Elizabeth on the right, run parallel with each other to Government House. These avenues are flanked by some of the oldest buildings in Port Louis. Others have been converted into modern buildings such as the Chamber of Agriculture offices and the sugar industry's headquarters of Plantation House.

Government House consisted originally of a wooden hut covered with palm tree leaves. Part of the building was constructed during the governorship of Nicolas de Maupin (1729-1735) and enlarged in 1738 by Labourdonnais when it was officially called the Hôtel du Gouvernement. The first British governor, Robert Townsend Farquhar, extended it still further. Today it is the official centre of government although parliamentary issues are debated in the modern Legislative Assembly Chamber behind it. In the courtyard is a statue of Queen Victoria which in summer time is shaded by the crimson blooms of a flamboyant tree. Beyond it is the statue of William Stevenson, who was the British governor of Mauritius from 1857 to 1863. The wrought iron gates in front of Government House remain closed except on official occasions such as the opening of parliament. The interior is not open to the public.

Opposite Government House are two statues. The statue of Sir John Pope Hennessy who was the British governor from 1883 to 1889, is the work of Mauritian sculptor, Maurice Louneau. Hennessy established a telephone service in Port Louis and installed electric lighting for the Civil Hospital. Believing that Mauritius should be for the Mauritians he gave them more responsibility and made himself unpopular with English officials. He spent the last year of his administration encouraging agriculture and tea cultivation.

The statue of Port Louis born barrister, Sir William Newton (1842-1915) stands beside Hennessy. After studying in England he returned to successfully defend Hennessy who was suspended following a commission of enquiry into the way he governed Mauritius. In

1889 Newton was elected Councillor of Port Louis.

To the right of Government House, on the corner of La Chaussée and Intendance Street, are the **Treasury Buildings** dating back to 1883. Built of stone and wood with an overhanging first floor verandah they house the offices of the Ministry of Works and the State Commercial Bank. Directly opposite is the Hong Kong and Shanghai Bank.

Next door to the Treasury Buildings along La Chaussée is the **Mauritius Institute** whose origins go back to 1880. It actively promotes the arts and culture and in this context operates four museums: the Naval Museum at Mahebourg, the Sir Seewoosagur Ramgoolam Memorial Centre for Culture in Port Louis, the Sookdeo Bissoondoyal Museum at Tyack and the Robert Edward Hart Museum at Souillac. Application to photograph exhibits at the Naval Museum should be made to the Director of the Mauritius Institute (see the Additional Information section at the end of this chapter).

Just in front of the Mauritius Institute, a magnificent Indian baobob tree flanked by two cannons, is set in a lawned garden. The cream two storied building houses the **Natural History Museum** on the ground floor. It is undergoing extensive refurbishment and only

---

Government House, at Port Louis

one section containing exhibits of marine flora and fauna is open. Eventually exhibits of the dodo and its cousin, the solitaire of Rodrigues will be on show. Exhibitions on culture and art are held here from time to time.

On the second floor the **National Library,** which is open to the public, contains 50,000 books and reference works and a substantial collection of magazines and periodicals. The museum and library are closed on Thursdays.

Continuing along La Chaussée is the sylvan setting of **Company Gardens** where settlers of the French East India Company had their original headquarters. In Labourdonnais' time it was no more than a marshy gulley where the dead were buried in a cemetery of the worst possible description. Port Louis suffered three dreadful cyclones in 1771 and 1773 followed by an outbreak of smallpox. The cemetery was ransacked by pigs who rooted out corpses and wandered the streets with rotting flesh. The authorities had long wanted to transfer the site of the cemetery to the outskirts but the clergy opposed it until Governor Desroches, ignoring their accusations of irreverance to the dead, ordered that the bodies be transferred to the western suburb of Cassis.

Two recumbent lions mark the entrance to the gardens. Inside there are many trees of botanical interest, the giant banyan tree with huge aerial roots and some lovely bottle palms. At lunch times Mauritians eat packed lunches or stroll along the cool pathways seeking respite from the city's heat. There are public toilets and a kiosk selling local handicrafts made by the Handicap Society. A stroll through the gardens gives the visitor an insight into Port Louis' historical past for it is here that statues of its famous sons are found.

The statue of Remy Ollier (1816-45) graces the entrance. A former teacher and trader he made his name as a journalist championing the struggle of the coloured population against slavery and campaigned for the establishment of a Port Louis Municipality.

Next is the statue of Adrien d'Epinay (1794-1839). He was an eloquent politician and lawyer who established the right wing newspaper *Le Cernéen*. When the abolitionists from England arrived, he represented the views of the sugar planters who maintained that they would be brought to economic ruin if slavery was abolished without compensation. His body is buried at Pamplemousses Cemetery. At the rear of the gardens is the statue of poet and journalist Leoville l'Homme (1857-1928) and the founder and editor of several prominent newspapers of the time.

Cross the road to Manilal Doctor Square to reach the second half of Company Gardens. On the left is the petite statue of Manilal

Doctor (1881-1956) under which is inscribed 'He felt for the oppressed and served them.' He came from India in 1907 at the request of Mahatma Ghandi to involve himself in the political and social problems of the Indo-Mauritians. Two years later he founded the first Indian newspaper *The Hindustani*.

On the right is the statue of Charles Edouard Brown-Sequard (1817-94), after whom a psychiatric hospital in Beau Bassin is named. He was a prominent doctor and psychiatrist who made fundamental discoveries in the field of human physiology. In 1864, after his election as a honorary doctor to the National Hospital, he was made a Fellow of the Royal Society of London. In 1869 the title of Knight of the Legion of Honour was conferred upon him.

An obelisk nearby commemorating the 141st anniversary of the abolition of slavery bears a plaque in Creole. It was dedicated to friends and victims of slavery and erected by the Federation Organisation Fraternelle on 13 April 1976.

The only monument erected in memory of a woman is that of Soeur Marie Barthelemey. She was a missionary who worked with cholera victims. The Chinese community with whom she also worked erected a monument to her at the Western Cemetery.

Walk up Intendance Street to the right of Government House to reach the **Port-Louis Theatre** situated in Nelson Mandela Square (Gillet Square). Designed by the French architect, Pierre Poujade, the theatre was completed in 1822 and contributed greatly to the city's cultural life. In the years preceding World War II, visiting French troupes performed plays and opera but it is rarely used these days save for the occasional stage show or hired out for wedding receptions. It is permanently locked although visits can be arranged to view the interior through the tourist office in Port Louis.

Directly opposite, in a flower-bedecked Creole building, is the old established store called Poncini, which sells quality imported gifts and above it are the premises of the Swiss Embassy.

Beyond the Municipal Theatre in Koenig Street is **City Hall** whose opening coincided with city status being granted on Port Louis by HM Queen Elizabeth II on 25 August 1966. Outside the building a spiral concrete walkway, rather like a fireman's training staircase, leads to a clock tower. It was constructed to symbolise the days when watch towers were erected over Port Louis to warn the inhabitants of outbreaks of fire. Across the road from City Hall, on the corner of Sir Seewoosagur Ramgoolam Street (Desforges Street) is the high rise modern Emmanuel Anquetil building which houses government offices and the Tourist Office.

Continue along Sir Seewoosagur Ramgoolam Street to Plaine

Verte where opposite the fuel station is a small wooden house hidden by high brick walls. Doctor Maurice Curé, one of the founders of the Labour Party was born here and the house was occupied by Sir Seewoosagur Ramgoolam between 1936 and 1965. Revered by all Mauritians as the 'Father of the Nation' and the architect of their independence from Britain, he died in 1985. Two years later the house was declared a National Monument and converted into a museum when it became known as the **Sir Seewoosagur Ramgoolam Memorial Centre for Culture**.

A bust of the great man stands in the shaded courtyard. In the house there are displays of his surgical instruments and medical diplomas although he never practised as a doctor. In another room a glass cabinet displays items of his clothing, some photographs and a stamp collection of first day covers commemorating events of his life. Amongst the photographs is one taken at the Maheswarnath Temple at Triolet when he became Chief Minister in 1961.

Clothing and souvenirs are slightly cheaper in Port Louis than in the plateau towns and substantially cheaper than the hotel boutiques. Bargains are found in the open-air market beside Victoria Square Bus Station and the Municipal Market. Window displays tend to be a jumble of wares but most shopkeepers willingly show their merchandise on request. Half the fun of visiting the city is to look, chat and barter, if necessary, with shopkeepers and stallholders who most of the time speak English. There is something for everyone in this higgledy-piggledy city: Pick and Buy in Sir Celicourt Antelme Street is a well stocked European style supermarket selling local and imported goods at reasonable prices while Mikado in Sir William Newton Street specialises in jewellery, shells, handicrafts, watches, souvenirs and French perfume. Arc en Ciel at the junction with Farquhar and Sir William Newton Street has a good selection of beachwear. Ocean Queen in Queen Street sells locally made articles and gifts. Inexpensive men's shirts catering for all tastes are widely available at shops in and around Sir Seewoosagur Ramgoolam Street (Desforges Street).

Lunch is taken as early as 11am when city workers down pens and either queue for *dholl puris* or take a more leisurely break in Creole, Chinese or Indian restaurants. Restaurants are generally cheaper than in Europe and most can provide European food of an excellent standard. They range from the simple to the sophisticated but very few remain open at night. It is impossible to list all eating places in the city but those that have been visited are mentioned below.

There are numerous snack bars in the Victoria Square Bus Station area. The old Tandoori Hotel provides lunches and makes a convenient base to people-watch while waiting for a bus. La Crabe d'Or in Barracks Street would go unnoticed were it not for its colourful sign of a crab suspended from the first storey. The restaurant overlooks the street and offers a wide range of simple and cheap Chinese food.

The only European-style café in Port Louis is La Flore Mauricienne in Intendance Street with tables and chairs set on a patio overlooking the street. It is popular with businessmen and tourists at lunchtime. There is an air-conditioned restaurant on the ground floor and a self service section in the basement. Snacks and drinks are served all day in a leisurely, unhurried atmosphere. It closes at 4pm.

The Shamrock at the junction with Corderie and Royal Road has an air-conditioned first floor restaurant making it a popular business venue. Specialities include Shamrock fried rice and chow mein. It is one of the few restaurants that remain open until 9pm.

The Rocking Boat Pub at the rear of La Bonne Marmite Restaurant in Sir William Newton Street, is Port Louis' only pub and its air conditioning provides welcome relief from the oppressive heat of the city. It is not a tourist attraction but a genuine attempt to provide business visitors with a slice of home fare. The atmosphere is relaxed and European with subdued lighting, wooden panels and beams. A well stocked bar serves local and imported drinks and draught beer. Substantial snack lunches are supplied by the adjacent Bonne Marmite kitchen. It closes around 7pm or when the last customer leaves.

La Cambuse Restaurant in St George Street is a delightful lunch-time venue with a picturesque courtyard and an interior giving the impression of being inside a galleon with a mural of a swashbuckling pirate complete with moll. Rickety wooden furniture, uneven wooden floors, hanging ropes and nets complete the nautical ambience. It closes at 4pm.

La Palmeraie in Sir Celicourt Antelme Street is a bamboo and shrub-clad restaurant cleverly set in an alleyway between two buildings with an unobtrusive entrance. It specialises in European cuisine and seafoods served in an intimate atmosphere.

La Bonne Marmite also closes at 4pm. It tends to be expensive but may be considered reasonable as the standards of food and service are high in elegant surroundings.

Carri Poulet on the Duke of Edinburgh Avenue serves arguably the best Indian cuisine. Expensive but of a higher standard and cheaper than comparable hotel restaurants the service is excellent. It is occasionally open in the evenings. On Wednesdays and Fridays there is a self-service buffet which is enormously popular and reservations are recommended. Kwang Chow is a restaurant at the junction with Queen Street and Anquetil Street. It is spacious and there are alcoves for private dining. The restaurant is open from 9.30am to 11pm.

Lai Min in Royal Road within walking distance of L'Amicale Casino is decorated with polished black floors, red and green paintwork and a model of a ferocious dragon in one corner. Mirrored walls enhance the spaciousness and gigantic fans divide the dining areas. A varied and extensive menu provides the finest Chinese cuisine. Specialities to order are worth the extra cost. It is open from 9am to 10pm.

The highlight of any visit to Port Louis is the **Central Market** where the oriental atmosphere of an old island port prevails. Here Muslim traders in flowing white robes, swarthy-skinned Indians and Chinese and colourful Creoles stand alongside shouting their wares to passers-by. The entrance to the market is via Farquhar Street, one block back from the harbour through wrought iron gates. The gates, built in 1844, are crowned with iron whorls and scrolls in which are inserted the initials VR after Queen Victoria. The market is noisy, hot and smelly throughout the day with customers wending their way through carpets of tropical produce and conical mounds of pungent herbs and spices. Stallholders douse fruit and vegetables with buckets of water in attempts to keep the flies off and their wares looking fresh. The market has a fish and meat section (not for the squeamish) and a bazaar where tourists can linger, look and barter for anything from beachwear, baskets and *bombli*, the dried salt fish with a stench that defies description. The stalls have something for everyone, whether it be a souvenir, a fresh fruit or a herbal remedy guaranteed to cure all ailments from diabetes to diarrhoea. The market opens at 6am everyday including Sundays.

The **Chinese Quarter**, located to the north of the market is the most colourful part of the city with its specialist food and spice shops bedecked in Chinese hieroglyphics. There are plenty of 'hotels' which should not be confused with accommodation. The Hotel Ding Dong, for example, is a restaurant specialising in Chinese food and elderly Mauritians still speak of going to the 'hotel' to eat.

The **Amicale Casino**, on the corner of Royal Road and Anquetil Street, is Port Louis' only source of night-time entertainment. Entrance is free, dress is informal and no passport is required. Security is provided by happy-go-lucky uniformed policemen who diplomatically ensure that the signs prohibiting photography are complied with. In the foyer, faded photographs of celebrities are pinned above an aquarium while ornate Chinese lanterns glint in the smoke-charged atmosphere. Throughout the day and well in to the night, pavement cooks or *bouillon trottoirs* squat on the streets outside the casino selling Chinese snacks or the colloquially termed 'hippy lunches' from steaming buckets of broth to hungry businessmen, bankers, diplomats and dockers. Occasionally an adventurous tourist can be seen supping much to the delight of the locals. Bowls and chopsticks are supplied but the pernickety can bring their own.

❄   The **Jummah Mosque**, incongruously situated in the heart of the Chinese Quarter in Royal Road, resembles an intricately iced oblong celebration cake, perched above a medley of tumbledown shops. Built around 1850 for the growing Muslim community it is the island's largest mosque and is a place of meditation rather than a tourist attraction. The main door is carved from teak and tourists are not normally allowed to enter beyond the courtyard. During Eid-El-Fitr, a festival of major spiritual importance signifying the end of Ramadam, hundreds of devotees repair to the mosque. Photographing the building is permitted but is likely to be frowned upon.

   Of interest to visiting yachtsmen and those with an interest in
❄ naval affairs is the **Merchant Navy Club**. It is situated to the right of the mosque in Joseph Rivière Street and is recognisable by the blue and white sign outside. Built in 1856 the large house is hidden behind high white walls and set in shady gardens of mimosa trees. A steward serves drinks and light snacks between 9am and 1pm in the cool wooden floored bar. There is a library of old books and magazines and comfortable chairs on a balcony that overlooks the front lawn. To the rear is an open courtyard with facilities for open-air cinema, table tennis, snooker table and more shaded seating areas. A notice warns that the club is not a mission but a multi-cultural, multi-faith establishment for seafarers and their guests although unaccompanied visitors may sometimes get permission to look around.

   On the waterfront is another national monument, the **General Post Office**. It was completed in 1868 when Sir Henry Barkly was governor. Postal services began in 1842 and improved greatly with the introduction of the railway 15 years later. The lines ceased operating in 1964 and many post offices are former railway stations, including the post office in nearby Victoria Square Bus Station.

   Across the road from the General Post Office is the Cafeteria du Port, an original storehouse dating back to the mid-nineteenth century looking distressingly decayed with its outer walls plastered with advertising stickers. The interior has been converted into a jumble of shabby shops looking out of place next to the well maintained buildings and statues of Place d'Armes nearby.

   Take the first road on the right from Place d'Armes along President J.F. Kennedy Street where the modern complex of Rogers House houses a vaccination centre, a branch of the Mauritius Commercial

Bank and most diplomatic missions, airline and shipping offices. Overseas calls may be made from the Overseas Telephone Service counter on the ground floor.

Line Barracks, built squarely around a central courtyard in Jemmapes Streets, are fine examples of early French colonial architecture. They were constructed by Antoine-Marie Desforges-Boucher, the last governor of the French East India Company before Mauritius was sold to the crown in 1764. Until then soldiers and sailors were billeted in private houses but their over familiarity with citizens led to such a breakdown in discipline that he was forced to build a proper barracks.

Today they straddle several blocks and house the Police Headquarters, Police Helicopter Unit and the Passport and Immigration Office. The entrance is in Jemmapes Street and public access is unrestricted. Opposite the Passport and Immigration Office is a legacy of British colonialism in the form of The Blue Lantern Police Clubhouse complete with a cardboard cut-out of a British bobby and gates with the words above it, 'Gateway to Charity'.

The **Champs de Mars**, cradled by the Moka Mountains, at the eastern edge of the city was a training ground for French soldiers. In 1812 it was converted into a race track by Colonel Edward Draper, an English army officer, whose passion for horse racing led to the founding of the Mauritius Turf Club. The race track is the oldest in the southern hemisphere. It was and still is a favourite promenade for the inhabitants of Port Louis. Race meetings are held every Saturday afternoon from the first week in May to the end of November when the grounds swell with the elite of the racing world, hopeful punters, knowledgeable pundits and followers of fashion. The Champs de Mars is also the venue for the annual Independence Day celebrations held on 12 March. The ceremony is presided over by the Prime Minister, politicians and diplomats and the public are entertained to a free cultural programme of singing and dancing.

There are two national monuments in the grounds of Champs de Mars: an obelisk in memory of the French Governor, Malartic, which was blown down during the terrible cyclone of 1892 and re-erected the following year and the statue of Edward VII the work of Mauritian sculptor, Prosper d'Epinay in 1912.

Nearby in Pope Hennessy Street is Mauritius' oldest hotel. The **National Hotel**, built in 1925, was owned by an old established Franco-Mauritian family for many years and in its heyday was used as a reception hall for the elite. Visiting troupes from France lodged in the rooms upstairs. The restaurant is open for lunch with a regular business clientele and food is good and remarkably cheap.

From the remparts of **La Citadelle** (also known as Fort Adelaide) there are panoramic views of the entire city with its amphitheatre of mountains, the Champs de Mars Race course and the harbour. The fort was named after Queen Adelaide, wife of William IV and built between 1834 and 1840 as a lookout post to check civil disorder within the city. Limited parking space is available with a security guard in attendance. For many years the fort was abandoned and fell into ruin but more recently it had been the venue of pop concerts and sound and light shows.

A stroll through quiet streets from the busy centre leads past delightfully restored Creole houses to Mere Barthelmey Street and uphill to the peaceful setting of **Marie Reine de la Paix**. It is situated on the flank of Signal Mountain and from its wide paved walkway there are breathtaking views of the city.

Erected just after World War II, Marie Reine de la Paix has always been a place of pilgrimage. In October 1989, thousands of islanders attended the mass celebrated by Pope John Paul when he made his first official visit to Mauritius.

It is possible to drive up **Signal Mountain** by taking Labour donnais Street south from the junction with St Georges Street. At the

The Chinese Quarter in Port Louis

top of St Georges Street is the picturesque La Patrimoine Guest House which is the only place in Port Louis where refreshments can be taken on Sundays. At the end of Labourdonnais Street the road rises up the flanks of the mountain and narrows in parts but the drive is worth the effort. From the small parking area there are different views of the capital, spreading inland in neat blocks to the foot of the Moka Mountains with the flatlands of the north in the distance. To the west there are views of Grand River North West and the filao-fringed headland of Pointe aux Sables. A very steep path to the summit of Signal Mountain leads to the radio transmitter station.

The **Chinese Pagoda**, a little drab and isolated, lies at the foot of Signal Mountain on the corner of Generosity and Justice Streets. A more colourful Chinese temple, bedecked with ornate scripts of names of sponsors, is located on the north side of Champs de Mars on the corner of Dr Eugene Laurent and Corneille Streets. Sandal-wood scent drifts from the red and gold interior where intricately carved deities evoke a mystic atmosphere. The oldest temple in Port Louis is the **Kwan Tee Temple** on the corner of Kwan Tee and Eugene Streets to the west of the city. Kwan Tee is venerated by the Chinese as a warrior god who fought for justice. Bank notes at the entrance are deposited by the faithful and burnt at funerals and memorial services as 'burial money'.

The **Church of the Immaculate Conception** on the corner of St George Street and Mère Barthelemey Street was formerly occupied by a small house where meetings were held by a Reverend Jacques Lebrun. He was sent to Mauritius by the London Missionary Society in 1814 to catechise the black population. The church was originally constructed of wood but had to be completely rebuilt following cyclone damage in 1892. Outside the church is a monument to the local reverend and his companions who died when their boat caught fire on a voyage to Reunion in December 1924.

St Louis Cathedral, in Cathedral Square, was consecrated in 1935 and is the third church to stand on this site. Under the French, it was a wooden structure called the Parochial Church of St Louis and was the only place of worship in the capital. Cyclones reduced it to a crumbling heap of ruins and it was reconstructed under Governor Farquhar in 1813. A report in 1925 revealed that the walls were infested with lizards and was such a danger that it had to be demolished and rebuilt. The present structure is similar in style to the original cathedral. The remains of Madame Labourdonnais and her son lie in the chapel known as Ames du Purgatoire.

The fountain outside the cathedral dates back to 1786. In those days drinking water had to be channelled from the heights of Pouce

Mountain where it eventually disgorged itself from the mouths of the four bronze lions around the fountain. The cross behind it was known as a 'depot' where corpses were placed for collection during the smallpox and cholera epidemics. Between the cathedral and the fountain is a statue of St Louis which was presented by the Mayor at the close of the nineteenth century. The Festival of St Louis (25 August) is an annual event celebrated by Roman Catholics from all over the island.

To the left of the cathedral is the **Episcopal Palace**, a fine nineteenth-century colonnaded mansion with high ceilings and wide verandahs.

The Anglican **St James Cathedral** in Poudriere Street was built on the site of an old gunpowder store which accommodated English prisoners of war. It was hastily turned into a church under the British in 1812 but was not completed until 1850 when it was consecrated. The bell belonged to the French governor, Magon, who owned the sugar estate at Villebague. Governor Farquhar had the bell transferred to Port Louis where it was installed in the belfry. During cyclones inhabitants would shelter within the precincts of the cathedral certain that they would be safe behind its 3m (10ft) thick walls.

The **Church and Shrine of Père Laval** at Sainte Croix to the northeast is only a short taxi ride or bus journey from Port Louis. If driving head north from Port Louis along the motorway to the first roundabout signposted for Tombeau Bay. Here take the third exit marked Ste Croix and drive for about 2km (1 mile) turning right at the next T-junction. Take the first turning left which is only about 50m (164ft) along and follow the road straight into Ste Croix.

Père Laval arrived as a missionary in 1841 and fought a long campaign to better the plight of the poor and sick. When he died in 1864 his body was buried in the graveyard of the old Church of Ste Croix and became the object of pilgrimage. He was beatified in 1979 and many still believe in his special healing powers.

The church was built to replace the original one and was consecrated in 1968. Set in the tranquil foothills of Long Mountain with views of L'Echelle Rock (The Ladder) to the south, the church is built on futuristic lines and with its lovely stained glass windows depicts scenes from the life of Christ. Outside the church in a modern, spacious vault a stone sarcophagus contains the remains of Père Laval beneath an effigy framed with flowers. Everyday hundreds of people of all faiths visit the tomb and pray to the sick. An annual pilgrimage takes place during the nights of the 7 and 8 September when thousands attend mass at the Church of Ste Croix. A special mass was held by the Pope when he made his official visit to

Mauritius in 1989.

At the rear of the church is a small museum depicting the life of Père Laval and some of his personal clothing is dispayed. Next door a shop sells religious postcards, books and souvenirs. The curate's residence nearby is a superb example of colonial architecture.

In the western suburbs of Port Louis is the **St Sacrament Church** **of Cassis**. Its fine Gothic structure was financed privately by a wealthy physician, Doctor Thomy d'Arifat. He died before the church was completed in 1879. Intended for the wealthy citizens of Port Louis it became known as the Cathedral of the Poor following their exodus to the plateau towns. It looks strangely out of place amongst the newer buildings nearby, notably the space age capsule construction of the Overseas Telecommunications Services Company where overseas telephone calls can be made 24 hours a day.

Robert Edward Hart Gardens contain two national monuments: one is a huge statue of Lenin's head and a monument in the form of an anchor which commemorates the French landing by Dufresne d'Arsel in 1715. The gardens are pleasant for walking in. The **Western Cemetery**, in the foothills of Signal Mountain contains tombs dating back to the mid-nineteenth century, some of are declared national monuments. Just outside the cemetery is a cenotaph dedicated to the people who died in the 1892 cyclone. It was one of the worst Mauritius had ever known with gusts of 216kph (134mph) which claimed the lives of 1,100 people and thoroughly wrecked dwellings and crops.

The industrial zone of Plaine Lauzanne lies on the Port Louis-Plaisance motorway. On the left a well-signposted slip road leads to the suburb of **Bell Village** where cultural centres stand side by side. The long established **Alliance Francaise** actively promotes the arts and French culture. Next door is the **African Cultural Centre** which houses a library and documentation unit. From time to time visiting and local song and dance troups entertain throughout the island. Details are advertised in the local press.

The finest building of all is the stunning pagoda of the **China Cultural Centre**. The non-governmental institution is accredited to Mauritius by the China Association for Cultural Exchange with Foreign Countries and its aims are to promote mutual understanding by cultural exchange. Visitors are welcome to look inside and/or attend the centre's cultural activities. It is particularly active in the field of song, dance, music and art.

Domaine les Pailles, situated in the foothills of the Moka Range is signposted left off the motorway after Bell Village. The estate occupies 3,000 acres where visitors can either walk or tour the grounds in horse drawn open topped carriages passing a reconstruction of and early sugar factory, windmill, rum distillery, spice garden and riding stables. A children's corner for the over 5's provides activities and entertainment including pony rides. Adults can make an adventurous safari in Land Rovers along 11km (7 miles) of winding mountain tracks through nature reserves containing wild stag, hare and monkey. A lodge some 336m (1,200ft) above sea level provides refreshment and wonderful views. Gourmet and vegetarian lunches and dinners can be taken at Le Clos Saint Louis Restaurant, a replica of an enormous colonial mansion while La Cannelle Rouge, provides simpler meals. A shop sells local agricultural produce, walking equipment, souvenirs and postcards. Night safaris followed by a candlelight dinner are available by arrangement.

Port Louis' hotel accommodation is more geared to short stay independent travellers. The City Hotel (formerly The Ambassador) in Sir Seewoosagur Ramgoolam Street is the most centrally located but can be noisy as it overlooks the main thoroughfare and is within earshot of the mosque. Near Victoria Square Bus Station is the Tandoori Tourist Hotel, above the restaurant which shares the same name, with bed and breakfast and private facilities. The Bourbon

The China Cultural Centre at Bell Village

Tourist Hotel in Jummah Mosque Street offers sixteen double rooms with private facilities and breakfast, bar and restaurant. Basic rooms are also available at France Tourist Hotel in Rivière Street and Palais d'Or in Jummah Mosque Street. Le Rossignol Hotel in Pope Hennessy Street has a downstairs restaurant and offers bed and breakfast with private facilities. None of these hotels approach the standards of the beach hotels or of the Gold Crest in Quatre Bornes or the Continental in Curepipe.

Additional Information

Amicale Casino
Royal Road
Open: every day from 7pm till around 2am.

City Hall
Koenig Street
Incorporates public library
☎ 208 0831
Open: Monday to Friday 9am-4pm.

Company Gardens
La Chaussée
Open: 7am-8pm.

Domaine les Pailles
Pailles
☎ 212 4225
Open: Monday to Saturday 9.30am-5.30pm. Night safaris and evening meals by arrangement with management.

La Citadelle
Overlooking Port Louis
Open: year round. For details of special events consult Mauritius Government Tourist Office in Port Louis.

Mauritius Institute and Natural History Museum
La Chaussée
☎ 212 0639
Open: Monday to Friday, 9am-

4pm. Saturday 9am-12noon. Closed Thursday, Sunday and public holidays. Admission free.

Père Laval Museum
Sainte Croix
Open: every day 9am-4pm.
Admission free.

Sir Seewoosagur Ramoolam Memorial Centre for Culture
SSR Street
Open: Monday to Friday, 9am-4pm. Saturday 9am-12noon. Closed Thursday, Sunday and public holidays. Admission free.

Bell Village
African Cultural Centre
Open: Monday to Friday 9am-4.30pm.

Alliance Francaise
Open: Monday to Friday 9am-4.30pm.
☎ 208 8648 or 212 2949

Chinu Cultural Centre
Open: Monday to Friday 9am-4.30pm. Saturday 9am-12noon.

Useful Addresses

CAR HIRE
Avis
Almadina Street
☎ 208 1624 or 208 6031

Europcar
Pailles
☎ 208 6054

Hertz Maurtourco
c/o Mauritius Travel and Tourism
    Bureau
Rue Royale
☎ 208 2041

EMERGENCIES
Dr A G Jeetoo Public Hospital
Volcy Pougnet Street
☎ 212 3201

Police Headquarters and Immigra-
    tion Department
Line Barracks
Jemmapes Street
☎ 208 1212

Passports and Immigration
    Department
Open: Monday to Friday 10am-
12noon and 1-2.30pm. Saturday's,
10-11.30am.

TOURIST INFORMATION
Mauritius Government Tourist
    Office
Emmanuel Anquetil Building
Sir Seewoosagur Ramgoolam Street
☎ 201 1703

6
THE PLATEAU TOWNS

The administrative district of Plaines Wilhelms rises gradually from the southern outskirts of Port Louis to a central plateau where the towns of Rose Hill, Beau Bassin, Quatre Bornes, Vacoas, Phoenix and Curepipe are situated. These towns are a little more than one hundred years old and are heavily populated.

In the early days of settlement, nobody dared to leave their homes on the coast and venture into the interior without an escort of soldiers. Much of it was unexplored and roads were often booby-trapped by runaway slaves. In 1721, the French found a German called Wilhelm Lechenig leading the life of a recluse in Plaines Wilhelms which is probably named after him. By the end of the eighteenth century only the lower part of Plaines Wilhelms was inhabited mainly by people fleeing from malaria in Port Louis. Between 1866 and 1888 cyclone, fire and disease swept the capital, forcing a second departure of its citizens to settle permanently in the healthier and safer uplands.

Curepipe was amongst the first towns to be settled, mainly by the white population, along with the suburbs of Vacoas, Phoenix and Floreal. Rose Hill, Beau Bassin and Quatre Bornes were inhabited by the upper and middle class coloured population and the freed Creole slaves led quiet fishermen lives on the coasts. Such divisions were by individual choice since there were no laws prohibiting residence to any one ethnic or social group although trains, introduced in 1864 with three separate classes, played a subtle role in encouraging segregation. The demise of the railway and the advent of classless buses removed segregationist tendencies and today Mauritians live and work together in almost perfect harmony.

Each town has its democratically elected municipal council or *municipalité*, which is responsible for the maintenance of roads,

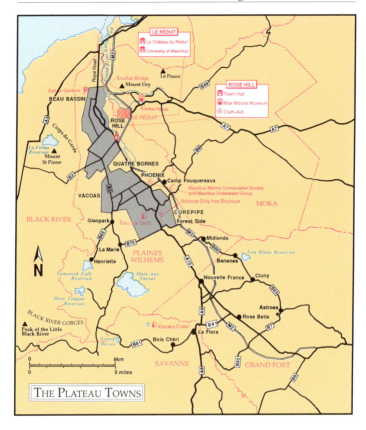

buildings and public gardens, leisure and sporting facilities, rubbish disposal and the general well being of its inhabitants.

Buses from Victoria Bus Terminus in Port Louis provide regular services to all the towns and cease operating at around 10pm. If driving there are two routes south from the capital: the old Royal Road or Route Royale which sweeps through the towns, changing its name several times, Curepipe, and the fast motorway with clearly marked roundabouts that by-passes them and links with the airport.

The markets, shops, cheap guest houses, snack bars and restaurants of the plateau towns will appeal to the independent traveller or anyone simply seeking a change of scenery. Throughout the year temperatures are a few degrees cooler than those of the coasts.

Rose Hill is the only town with an Anglo Saxon name and was named after the rosy sunsets on the mountain of Corps de Garde. Beau Bassin (Beautiful Pond) is named after a fish pond experiment conducted by the Ministry of Agriculture. The towns have been linked since 1896 for administrative purposes but it was not until 1927 that the Town Hall of Rose Hill/Beau Bassin was built.

Coming from Port Louis, the **Town Hall** is situated on the right hand side of the main Royal Road before reaching Rose Hill town centre. On the lawn is a fountain and statue called La Fontaine des Arts which is the work of two local artists, Neermab Hurry and Serge Constantin. The Town Hall also houses the **Plaza Theatre** which opened in 1933 with the showing of a musical film *Le Lieutenant Souriant* (*The Smiling Lieutenant*) with Maurice Chevalier. It is the largest theatre in the Indian Ocean where plays and cultural events always attract an enthusiastic audience. The variety of the theatre's productions of opera, song and dance, emphasise the island's cultural diversity with performances in English, French, Creole and Indian languages. The enormously popular events are advertised in the local press and tickets are quickly sold out.

Attached to the theatre is the diminutive **Max Moutia Museum**, named after Rose Hill's famous post-war opera singer and music teacher. The museum is reminiscent of the foyer of an old established London theatre where posters of past productions and photographs of members of the 1930s Mauritius Dramatic Club evoke an atmosphere of its glamorous past. The Town Hall complex includes a library with a good Mauritiana reference section and the Max Boulle Art Gallery where works of local artists can be viewed.

It is well worth making a visit to **Craft-Aid** in Sir Edgar Laurent Street, a small non-profit industry which provides creative and remunerative employment for disabled people. To get there turn left outside the Town Hall and left again into Ambrose Street. Pass St Andrews College on the right. Two turnings on the right after the college is Sir Edgar Laurent Street where gates on the right indicate Craft-Aid. The project was started in 1983 by an Englishman, Paul Draper, who after much hard work, created Craft-Aid to help disabled people help themselves. Employees with varying disabilities are paid wages stipulated by the government and a bonus system enables them to earn more than the minimum wage. Visitors are warmly received and encouraged to inspect the workshop and goods. Craft-Aid publishes an annual newsletter of their work and a similar project has been started in Rodrigues.

A classic example of colonial architecture can be seen at **Maison Carné** on turning right outside the Town Hall. The house, empty and unoccupied, is set back off the Royal Road. It was owned by the Count and Countess de Carné and now belongs to the municipality. Occasionally there are exhibitions of colonial furniture and paintings. Continue towards Rose Hill centre and on the left is the 1941 built church of **Sacre Coeur de Montmartre**. On the right is the older 1890 built **Church of Notre Dame de Lourdes** with its statue of the Virgin Mary on a pedestal outside.

The Bus Terminus, at Place Cardinal Margeot, is built on European lines with wide bays, free toilets and public telephones. Connections to most parts of the island can easily be made from here. Queues are orderly in covered bus stands and bus routes are prominently displayed. Inspectors are helpful often personally ensuring that tourists are escorted to the correct bus.

The Post Office, near the bus terminus was the former railway station. Its Victorian solidity stands proud amidst the modern highrise buildings of the shopping centre. Between them are ubiquitous food stalls and snack bars and unlike Port Louis which shuts down after dark, Rose Hill is comparatively lively come evening.

Rose Hill has developed into one of the islands main shopping areas with new western style shops and arcades. Aviva is a modern department store that sells mostly goods from Europe and the Far East. The browsing shopper is requested to place personal belongings in a depository before entering the store and may feel scrutinised by over-attentive staff and security cameras.

Arab Town, across the road from the Post Office and named after the Muslim traders who gathered here to sell their wares, has also been refurbished. Neat Creole style stalls with pastel green corrugated roofs provide cover for modern merchants who display an array of basketware, beachwear and household goods.

Continue through Arab Town to the covered **Market**. Bright anthuriums grace an otherwise drab entrance where meat, fish, fruit and vegetables are displayed. Behind the market is the **Daar-us-Salaam Mosque** which was founded in 1923. The green and white building is adorned with fairy lights and a placard proclaiming 'Love for all. Hatred for none.'

The heart of Rose Hill is on Royal Road where long established shops are situated. Window shopping is quite an art and finding what you want from the jumble of wares takes time and patience. Of interest however, is the **Rose Hill Pharmacy** reminiscent of a Dickensian apothecary with old bottles of lotions and potions displayed on dark wooden shelves. The present is reflected by white coated knowledgeable assistants providing modern remedies. Nearby is the newly refurbished first floor offices of the British Council with its library and supply of current newspapers and magazines. Below is a depot of the Dry Cleaning and Steam Laundry Company but service can take several days. One Mauritian wit remarked to a passing tourist that Rose Hill's claim to fame was that it was the only town in the island where one could cleanse the body, mind and apparel by visiting the pharmacy, library and dry cleaners all in the space of a few yards!

Branches of main banks are located in Royal Road. The police station by the traffic lights on the corner of Royal Road and Moka Road has a telephone for public use.

From the bus station at Rose Hill take Vandemeersch Street to the first roundabout to reach **Beau Bassin.** In the centre of town, is the lovely 1880s built Church of Sacre Coeur and a small market and several banks. Taxis and public toilets can be found in the courtyard of the colonial style Police Station. Across the road is the Roxy Cinema and nearby a small quiet park provides seating beneath trees where locals take lunchtime snacks. Off the main road are residential streets, bordered by evergreens and old fashioned road signs, more reminiscent of an English village than a tropical suburb.

A short way beyond the Police Station is a delightful Boulangerie, Le Rallye, where freshly baked bread, cakes and pies are sold. For piping hot snacks, try the *samousas* and *gateaux piments*.

Balfour Gardens is a tranquil retreat and recreational area for the townsfolk. It is poorly signposted from Beau Bassin and the simplest way of getting there is to turn right at the first set of lights on Vandermeersch Street from Rose Hill into Swami Sivananda Street. Continue along this road for about $1^1/_2$km (1 mile) to supermarket on the left called Chez Estelle and a confectioners next door which sells slices of fruit cake and drinks. Across the road a small unimpressive sign marks the entrance of the gardens.

They were named after Dr Andrew Balfour, a sanitation expert from England, who arrived in Mauritius in 1921 and wrote of the lack of hygiene in Port Louis. Follow the main pathway to the thatch-roofed kiosk for all round views of the gardens where palm trees, tropical shrubs and flowers grow in profusion. At the rear of the gardens a large enclosure contains giant tortoises. Beyond it one may look across a ravine to a waterfall which tumbles into an enormous gorge where it flows into the Grand River North West to Port Louis. To the north there are views of the peaks of the Moka Range.

At the top of the ravine is a large white manor house originally known as La Tour Blanche (The White Tower). John Augustus Lloyd, an English army captain, built the house which included stables and the island's only elephant, as a second home for his family in 1834.

Two years later Charles Darwin reached Port Louis aboard the *HMS Beagle* and stayed as his guest for a few days. The area attracted the English aristocracy and diplomats, whose love for gracious living, horse riding and gardening quickly earned it the name of the English Quarter. In 1946 it became the residence of a Madame Dorothy Rouillard and her husband. They spent many happy years here until her husband died in 1969. Shortly before her death in 1977 the house was donated to the Catholic diocese of Port Louis. It was renamed **Le** **Thabor** and became a monastery. In 1983 it was transformed into a pastoral centre for the Church of Mauritius and Rodrigues and later completely refurbished to receive the Pope on his 1989 official visit.

The area of **Le Réduit**, less than 4km (2 miles) from Rose Hill is the centre of higher education. Take the B1 Moka road by turning left at the Police Station in Rose Hill passing the Mauritius Sugar Research Institute on the left and crossing the Grand River North West. At the roundabout after the bridge, is the sturdy College of Agriculture, founded in 1913 and the University of Mauritius. Nearby are the educational broadcasting offices of the College of the Air and the Mauritius Institute of Education.

 Le Château du Réduit, is clearly marked at the first exit of the roundabout. This magnificent two storied house is the official residence of the Governor General. A permanent police sentry allows access to the 325 acres (130 hectares) of gardens.

The château was built in 1748 by the French governor, Barthélemy David as a country residence and retreat for wives and children of the French East India Company in the event of invasion. He chose a site on a peninsular isolated by two deep ravines where two streams form the Grand River North West. The area was later called Le Bout du Monde (The End Of The World) from the way the peninsular tapered off into the depths of the ravine. The original wood structure of the château was damaged by cyclones but extensions were made by successive French and English governors. It is now almost entirely constructed in stone. Access to the interior is not permitted.

It was from Le Réduit that the governor's wife, Lady Gomm, unintentionally made philatelic history when she used the famous penny blues and twopenny orange postage stamps to send invitations to a ball. The stamps had been engraved by a Joseph Barnard who inadvertently engraved the words 'Post Office' instead of 'Post Paid'. One thousand stamps were issued and most of them were bought by Lady Gomm. They are highly treasured by philatelists.

The gardens contain exotic trees and shady pathways surrounded by creepers, ferns and flowers. Originally designed by the French botanist, Aubet, they contained fruit trees, spices, cotton and corn.

The awe-inspiring Cavadee is celebrated in January and March

Colourful Hindu festivals are celebrated year round

116 • Visitor's Guide: Mauritius, Rodrigues & Reunion

Later British governors landscaped the gardens and laid lawns. In 1813 rumours circulated Mauritius that it was about to be invaded by monstrous sea creatures following the discovery of a boa constrictor that had made itself comfortable in the gardens. The truth was that it had escaped from an Indian ship and armed men caught and killed it before transporting it to Port Louis for all to see.

Return to the roundabout and follow the signs for **Moka.** The area was named after the important coffee trading town on the Red Sea. The road links with a roundabout on the Port Louis motorway. Take the second exit to reach the **Mahatma Gandhi Institute**. It occupies 35 acres (14 hectares) of land and was set up as a joint venture between the Indian and Mauritian governments to promote Indian culture and to serve as an educational and cultural study centre. Within the complex is a secondary school, printing press and publications department, the School of Mauritian, African and Asian Studies and a newly established School of Indian Studies. An auditorium offers facilities for conferences and cultural programmes. Events are advertised in the local press.

By returning to the motorway at Rose Hill and heading in the direction of Port Louis an interesting detour can be made to the lovely old Creole house of **Eureka**. After 3km (2 miles) take the exit on the right which is signposted Montagne Orry and Moka. The road climbs steeply for half a kilometre and then bears right through an avenue of palm trees. The house is on the left.

The house was built in 1856 by an English gentleman who sold it to Eugene Leclezio, the first Mauritian Judge of the Supreme Court. A few years later it was put up for auction. His son, Henri Leclezio, the President of the Legislative Council and one of the island's most powerful and influential men, made a bid and cried 'Eureka' when his offer was accepted. Henceforth the house has been known as Eureka. Henri Leclezio devoted his life to restoring Eureka into a home which became the birthplace of his descendants. The grounds originally spread over 170 acres (68 hectares) with two houses and three pavilions and was privately occupied until April 1986 when the heirs turned part of it into a museum and opened it to the public.

Several influential Mauritians and companies contributed to the erection of the museum and their names are displayed outside. Eureka is set in the foothills of a soaring mountain where 5 acres (2 hectares) of lovely gardens tumble to the edge of an awesome ravine. Built entirely of indigenous wood it has 109 doors and occupies an area of 1,000sq m (10,758sq ft). Visitors may relax over tea on its huge verandah overlooking tranquil gardens. Creole lunches can also be served by arrangement with the management.

The Plateau Towns• 117

Inside the high-ceilinged rooms are beautiful examples of colonial furniture reflecting its gracious past along with photographs and models of Mauritian houses. In the gardens one of the original pavilions has been converted into a stamp and souvenir shop.

Superb views of the landward aspect of the Moka Range encircling Port Louis can be seen by turning right outside Eureka and right again at the next T-junction. Cross the Souillac Bridge over the River Moka and turn left on to the B46 where there are signs for Moka. Here majestic colonial mansions are hidden behind enormous bamboo hedges, including Val Orry, the former residence of Reza Khan Palavi, the ex-Shah of Iran.

The Moka road trails through untidy little villages to Nouvelle Decouverte. Just before reaching Roselyn Cottage, a signpost indicating the 818m (2,683ft) high Le Pouce mountain on the left leads through sugar cane fields. For closer views of the main peak of the Moka range, the Pieter Both at 934m (3,064ft), continue along the B49 to La Laura where a sign indicates right for Long Mountain and Nicolière and left for Rivière Baptiste. Take the left turn through cane fields where the peak of Pieter Both looms closer.

The first climb was made by a Frenchman, Claude Penthé on 8 September 1790 who celebrated the event by hoisting the tricolour on its peak. The story goes that during a second climb some 8 days after the first he fired a rifle to announce his presence. During the nineteenth century Port Louis residents would picnic in the foothills and the peak would attract adventurous mountaineers, including the American Consul, Nicholas Pike. Climbing the peak today should only be attempted by the experienced.

Return to the southbound carriageway of the Port Louis-Plaisance motorway to reach **Quatre Bornes**. The town is clearly marked with a 'Welcome to Quatre Bornes' sign at the St Jean roundabout on the motorway. The sombre Victorian built Catholic Church of St Jean lies slightly off the road with a convenient parking area. Yet more views of the Moka Range, which are particularly beautiful at sunset and sunrise, can be photographed from the roundabout.

Township status was granted in 1895. Quatre Bornes (Four Boundary Stones) was named after four former sugar estates denoted its original boundary. To the west is the unmistakable Corps de Garde Mountain at 720m (2,362ft) and to the south Candos Hill, a little hillock at 484m (1,588ft) that was once used for military target practice. When the island was under French occupation Corps de Garde served as a look out post for runaway slaves. Some Mauritians insist that it resembles the recumbent figure of the Unknown Soldier but this depends on the imagination of the observer.

The large Indian population is reflected in the number of temples around the foothills of Corps de Garde. In January, and March, the Tamil speaking Hindus observe Cavadee, the most dramatic of their religious ceremonies. Tourists are welcome to observe the spectacular acts of faith which are the outcome of weeks of fasting.

Permission to climb Corps de Garde must be obtained from the Forestry Department as the area is a designated nature reserve. Mauritours and walking groups such as the government sponsored Randonnée du Coeur or the privately run Centre Excursion de Beau Bassin sometimes organise treks to the mountains.

Quatre Bornes centre at first appears uninspiring. Its shops and restaurants cater for its inhabitants at prices cheaper than those normally found in the tourist areas but its beauty lies in its residential streets which spread around the main road into a maze of bamboo-clad avenues. Here there are some beautiful traditional houses set in large gardens. The town is reputed for its flowers and the insignia on the Town Hall, 'Urbs Floris' is well justified with streets in the old quarter behind the market being named after flowers.

The town lays no claim to being a tourist attraction but provides an insight into Mauritian life. Well-stocked supermarkets attract locals from all over and the SPES Boutique in Labourdonnais Avenue offer good buys for tourists in unusual handicrafts and souvenirs. The market or *Foire* on Wednesdays and Saturdays, is a lively affair offering tropical fruit and vegetables, snacks, household goods and clothing beneath multi-coloured canopies.

The Bus Terminal at Place Koenig harbours an enthusiastic taxi service for guests staying at the Gold Crest Hotel, a popular base with visiting businessmen and tourists. At the rear of the hotel a cool arcade with modern shops and a self service restaurant is patronised by young Mauritians and hotel clients. Next door is Rolly's Steak House. The large white building almost opposite the Gold Crest Hotel houses the Town Hall and library.

The Happy Valley is a grand Chinese restaurant known for its authentic cuisine and good service with a choice of fixed menus or à la carte lunch and dinners. Other Chinese restaurants such as Chopsticks and the Singapore are less pretentious and cheaper.There are fast food outlets at the cafeteria at the rear of the Gold Crest Hotel and Mr Chef in St Jean Road. Both are open till late.

There is excellent take-away Chinese food at Ok Ling, 89 Celicourt Antelme Avenue near the junction with Leclezio Avenue. Known to the locals as Ti Garage (Little Garage), it is difficult to find but Quatre Bornes based taxi drivers should know it. Ok Ling's garage is situated two doorways after the permanently boarded-up Mine de

Chine restaurant. Business hours are erratic although the restaurant is usually open during the evenings.

Nightlife centres round The Palladium, a pseudo-Roman style building on the Port Louis motorway $1^1/_2$km (1 mile) north of the St Jean roundabout at Trianon. Here a discoteque, casino and restaurant provide all the ingredients for a late night out but arrange your own transport. Within walking distance from the Gold Crest Hotel, on the main road is the Alibi, a cosy, air-conditioned piano bar and restaurant which provides nightly entertainment.

Panoramic views over Quatre Bornes can be admired from **Candos Hill**, by taking the B3 south from Quatre Bornes centre and turning left at the traffic lights at La Louise junction in the direction of Vacoas and Curepipe. Turn left again opposite the Princess Margaret Orthopaedic Hospital and follow the road uphill through the new residential area of Sodnac. Here a large, modern housing complex clings to the hillsides in streets named after birds.

The next town from Quatre Bornes is **Vacoas**, named after the pandanus or vacoas tree that flourished here. It is a tree lined shaded area which is famous for market gardening. The cooler temperatures have traditionally attracted ex-patriates, diplomats and Franco-Mauritian businessmen. Vacoas and Phoenix have been linked since 1968 as one municipality.

For many years the British had a land based communications centre, HMS Mauritius at Vacoas. It formerly comprised barrack type accommodation and is now the headquarters of the Special Mobile Force (SMF). Its origins go back to 1960 when officers were trained to take over army duties previously undertaken by Kenyan troups stationed in Mauritius after World War II. There is no army but the force undergo rigorous SAS style training and is equipped to deal with sudden emergencies and public disorder though such instances have so far been rare.

The Gymkhana Club nearby was a polo club for officers in the mid-nineteenth century. It is now an 18-hole golf course and the includes a swimming pool, snooker room and club house. Temporary mem bership is available for visitors on a daily or monthly basis.

Eating places are scarce in Vacoas apart from along the main road. Also on Main Road is Sam's Disco which is open every night except Monday from 9pm and offers the latest ear-cracking pop and heavy rock music in the ground floor disco. Upstairs in La Plantation Piano Bar, an excellent local jazz trio perform late into the night in a sophisticated air-conditioned ambience and there are theme evenings. The venue is a popular late night haunt with locals and tourists but do arrange your own transport.

120 • Visitor's Guide: Mauritius, Rodrigues & Reunion

Phoenix is a mainly industrial area with large food and drinks processing companies and from where the popular Mauritian beer takes its name. Of special interest to underwater enthusiasts and marine conservationists, are the headquarters of the Mauritius Underwater Group in Railway Road. The headquarters can be approached by cutting through Vacoas but since there is a one way system it may be easier to take the route described below.

Drive south along the motorway from Port Louis as far as the roundabout which is clearly landmarked by the Phoenix Brewery on the left. Take the second exit and follow Avenue Dr Xavier Nalletamby which is a one way road running parallel to Railway Road. At the first crossroads turn right in front of St Columba's Church then first right and quickly right again to join Railway Road. About $^1/_2$km (500yd) on the right hand side of the road are the headquarters and clubhouse of the Mauritius Underwater Group in an unpretentious wooden hut flanked by a model of a shark, cannon and anchor. They share the premises with the Mauritian Marine Conservation Society.

The club was founded in 1964 and is affiliated to the British Sub Aqua Club. Temporary membership is available and allows use of club equipment and access to the clubhouse, conditional to evidence of proper documentation showing diving qualifications.

The Mauritius Marine Conservation Society holds regular meetings and slide shows at the clubhouse. It is a relatively new organisation set up to highlight awareness of damage to the coral reef. Its aims are to educate by the use of slide shows and lectures, carry out marine surveys and in due course establish marine parks. The society has produced a video film of its work and created reefs by sinking barges in areas where it has been destroyed.

Curepipe (pronounced 'cure-peep') is the highest plateau town at 550m (1,804ft) and is situated half way between Mahebourg and Port Louis. The popular story goes that soldiers used Curepipe to stop and clean or 'cure' their pipes during the long marches across the island while some historians maintain it was named after a village in south-west France. Whatever the truth, it is a popular place for shopping and offers an insight into the elite society of the Franco-Mauritians who have resided there since the 1860s. The residential streets are often nameless and in spite of an effort to introduce nameplates, they were mysteriously and systematically removed. Houses are unnumbered and are concealed behind tall bamboo hedges. Even with a map, getting around the town is frustrating.

The town holds the dubious distinction of having the highest rainfall on the island at 3m (120in) per annum. The topography of the area around the town and the height of nearby forestlands combine to produce micro-climates with the result that Curepipiens are continually bemoaning the fact that it always rains and they are rarely seen without an umbrella. So why go there? Even the most avid sunseeker could tire of hot sun, sea and sand, not to mention the mosquitoes which sometimes accompany them. A day spent wandering around under cool grey skies, liberated from the greasy film of insect repellant, can be quite a relief. Curepipe is also the gateway for an inspiring walk to the Black River Gorge.

A walk or taxi ride to the west of the town leads to a steep winding climb to **Trou aux Cerfs**. This crater, 300m (984ft) in diameter, was formed as a result of volcanic activity millions of years ago and is now choked with silt, water and a dense forest of vegetation. It is possible to scramble down the sides to the water level but caution is advised. There is plenty of parking and a kiosk to shelter walkers. There are spectacular views of the island: looking west the first majestic vista is Rempart Mountain which Mark Twain described as a 'vest pocket Matterhorn'. This is flanked to the right by the three peaks of Les Trois Mamelles, standing proud, as Mauritians say, like three breasts. To the north-west the humps of Mont St Pierre are dwarfed by the bulk of the Corps de Garde. In the foreground Candos Hill rises looking like a smooth mole hill. To the north lies the sprawl of Curepipe and Phoenix and in the distance Port Louis. Discernible by the jumbled range of the Moka Mountains, is the isolated peak of the thumb-like Pouce and the tiny ball forming the head of Pieter Both. Other peaks rise and fall like papier mache replicas dumped on the landscape by a child.

In the town there are several historic buildings. **Royal College** in Sir Winston Churchill Street, is opposite the Continental Hotel. Under the French it was known as the Lycée Colonial and was situated in Port Louis where most families lived at the end of the eighteenth century. Following cyclones and plague the college was hurriedly transferred to Curepipe in totally inadequate buildings in 1899. The present college was designed by French architect, Paul le Judge de Segrais and work began under the British in 1912. Amongst its teachers was Walter Besant who wrote of his experiences in Mauritius and Reunion in his *Bourbon Journal*. In front of the college is a statue of a French and British infantryman (the Poilu and the Tommy) dedicated to those who fell in World War I.

The **Town Hall**, in a delightful wooden Creole building, dates back to the end of the nineteenth century when Curepipe was given municipality status. The **Carnegie Library** nearby was named after Andrew Carnegie, the famous philanthropist. In 1912 an American

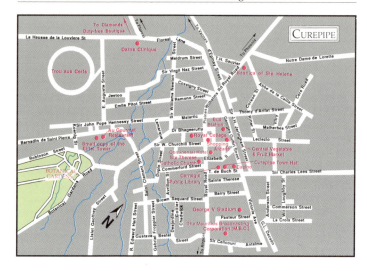

captain, Ross Bain who lived in Curepipe with his Mauritian wife, realised the need for a library in the town and wrote to the Carnegie Foundation. Following negotiations a donation of £1,800 was made and in 1920 the library opened to the public with 22,000 volumes of rare works and manuscripts on the Mascarene Islands.

The gardens surrounding the Town Hall contain a monument to the first French cartographer of Mauritius, Abbe de la Caille. His map served as a model to all subsequent maps of the island and copies of his work can be seen in the Mahebourg Naval Museum. Nearby is a bust of the French poet, Jean Paul Toulet and a bronze statue of Paul and Virginie, the ill-fated lovers of the *St Geran* shipwreck, whom Bernadin St Pierre described in his famous novel, *Paul et Virginie*.

There are two Roman Catholic churches in Curepipe. The awesome grey stone **Ste Therese Church** in the Royal Road was built by Abbey Comerford in 1868 and consecrated on Christmas Day 1872. The bell was designed by the French architect, Paul Marion de Proce. The **Basilica of Ste Helene** on the Plaines Wilhelms Road to the north of the town was built from funds given by Hélène Naz, whose father, Virgil, was a celebrated barrister and plantation owner.

Curepipe celebrated its centenary in 1989 and houses and shops were spruced up for the occasion. Curepipe's market was included in the facelift but even a coat of paint could not beautify the ugly concrete chimneys which rise like massive fog horns. Outside the ubiquitous *dholl puri* and *gateaux piments* stalls provide cheap snacks and the market, contains sections for meat, fish, poultry and exotic mounds of tropical fruit and vegetables.

But Curepipe is keeping up with the times. The Jan Palach Bus Station next door was built in 1990 to replace the old bus station that consisted of an assault course of gulleys and broken pavements that filled with muddy water every time it rained. However, Curepipe's varied shops continue to attract anyone in search of a special souvenir or present. Chinese shops sell ivory, porcelain and silk and Prisunic Supermarket stocks wines, cheeses and speciality foods freshly imported from France. Arcades Currimjee, below the Continental Hotel, provides refuge from sudden downpours and an opportunity for window shopping in some of the best and most expensive shops in Mauritius. Here two book shops, Librairie Allot and Librairie du Trefle, stock an extensive range of foreign language books, magazines and newspapers.

The **Botanical Gardens** are a quiet and exotic area to visit, and are permanently open. The entrance in Botanical Gardens Street, is adjacent to the offices of the Conservator of Forests where permission can be obtained to visit the nature reserves of the interior. In the small gardens beside his offices is a valuable collection of indigenous plants such as the boucle d'oreilles which have taken years of patient care to nurture. Nearby are azaleas and Australian bottlebrushes and other labelled specimens.

Occupying an area of 5 acres (2 hectares) Curepipe Botanical Gardens are much smaller than those at Pamplemousses. A quiet stroll stopping to admire the lakes, lawns and indigenous plants and trees, is a traditional Curepipien pastime and will appeal to horticulturists. The only guide to the gardens is *Le Jardin Botanique de Curepipe* by Guy Rouillard and Joseph Guehoe (1990). It is written in French and available from bookshops in Curepipe and Port Louis.

It is possible to drive through the gardens providing the speed limit of 16kph (10mph) is observed. The picking of any specimens is prohibited. The main entrance leads to Avenue Charles Baudelaire off which more avenues are named after local dignitaries. To the right is a kiosk erected in 1892 where military bands used to play music to the delight of residents on Sundays.

Of special interest, in Avenue Horne, is the only known example of the indigenous palm, *Hyophorbe amaricaulis*, found by accident, when the area was cleared to create the gardens. Amongst other specimens is the heart shaped viah palm, a member of the arum family from Madagascar which grows in an attractive lake. Beyond Avenue Horne to the west of the gardens is an enclosure containing indigenous trees including the rare bois d'olive, the tambalacoque and the bois de natte which are now protected species.

In keeping with other plateau towns, Curepipe lacks nightlife and were it not for the Casino de Maurice and several excellent restaurants, there would be little point in going there for an evening. The casino is situated at an unimpressive entrance at the rear of the Central Electricity Board. Entrance is free and no passport is required unless changing foreign money. Excursions to the casino and late night transport are often arranged through the hotels.

Restaurants and cafés are plentiful in the town. But for a really special lunch or dinner in truly colonial surroundings with a view of a miniature Eiffel Tower in its grounds, try the Au Gourmet Restaurant in Avenue St Bernadin. It is open lunchtimes and evenings but closed Saturday lunchtimes and Sundays. The house was built in 1889 as a private residence and part of it was converted into a restaurant specialising in French cuisine with a Creole touch by Madame Jacqueline Dalais, a Franco-Mauritian lady and Member of the Dames Cuisinières de France. It is acclaimed as one of the best restaurants in Mauritius and reservations are recommended.

Curepipe has its own brand of pensions and guest houses mainly catering for the independent traveller. The Continental Hotel, on the corner of Plaines Wilhelms Road and Châteauneuf Street, is a pleasant place to eat or drink and is centrally situated for the best shops and the suburbs of Forest Side and Floreal. Helpful drivers are available at the permanent taxi stand outside the hotel. Trips can be arranged either independently or through tour operators to visit the Adamas Duty Free Boutique at **Floreal.** This is a factory specialising in the cutting of diamonds where visitors can purchase duty free diamonds which can be collected at the airport on their departure or have jewellery made to order.

Excursions From Curepipe

Many people combine a shopping trip to Curepipe with a drive through Plaine Champagne and the Black River Gorges. Plaine Champagne is a good starting point to visit Macchabée-Bel Ombre Forest. The easiest way of getting there is to take the B70 south-west of Curepipe which sweeps through fields of sugar cane and tea plantations to La Marie.

The road passes along deep forest of pine and travellers palm to the natural lake of **Mare aux Vacoas** which is the island's largest reservoir. Its outlets have been damned to increase its water capacity to Plaines Wilhelms, parts of the west coast and Nouvelle France. The

The Plateau Towns• 125

water is treated at the nearby La Marie filter works.

Continue for 7km (4 miles) to a junction called **Le Pétrin** where there is easy access, by foot or car, to the breathtakingly beautiful reservoirs, mountains and forests. At Le Pétrin there is a small forester's hut and a placard showing a map of the walking trails to the Black River Gorge, Tamarin Falls and Mare Longue. There are no refreshment facilities so take your own food and water.

To the east of Le Pétrin is **Grand Bassin**, a lake occupying the centre of an extinct volcano and at 702m (2,303ft) the air is still and haunting. The banks are formed from basalt and lava and in the middle is a small islet. Underwater springs feed the lake and rains flowing from the surrounding mountains ensure that the level remains constant. It was popularly held that the lake was bottomless but the depth is about 20m (66ft). The waters are sacred to the Hindus who flock to the cluster of waterside temples each February to celebrate Maha Shivaratree. At other times they repair to the lake to offer thanks and pray while others sit on the little wooden benches overlooking the lake. The area is a pleasant place to picnic. An alternative way of returning to Curepipe can be made by continuing past Grand Bassin where the road drops and zigzags towards the tea plantations of Bois Chéri, Grand Bois and Nouvelle France.

At Bois Chéri a couple of kilometres from Grand Bassin, a small sign on the left indicates **Kanaka Crater** through rough tracks of tea plantations which from a distance look like thick strips of green corduroy. The tracks are not really suitable for vehicles but walkers may enjoy the 4¹/₂km (3 miles) hike to this extinct volcanic crater which rises steeply to some 208m (682ft).

South of Le Pétrin en route to Chamarel the road passes through **Plaine Champagne,** named after the creamy white flowers of the privet which resemble the white froth on a glass of champagne. The privet, like the Chinese guava from Brazil grow in such profusion here that they have invaded areas previously occupied by native forest. In winter locals gather the vitamin C rich cherry red fruits of the Chinese guava.

At Plaine Champagne there are three well marked viewpoints within 3km (2 miles) of each other giving views across the Black River Gorges. The first, 7km (4 miles) from Le Pétrin, is on the left and is marked 'Alexandra Falls' and leads through shaded forest. The second, 1km (¹/₂ mile) on, is closed to vehicles and entails a short walk along a well trodden but unmarked pathway. The third is marked 'Black River Gorges Viewpoint' where there is a parking area and a notice warning drivers not to leave vehicles unaccompanied. From here there are panoramic views across the gorges with the

Travellers Palms adorn the banks of most rivers on Mauritius

peaks of Rempart Mountain and Corps de Gards in the north-west just visible in the distance.

The area is the last refuge of some of the world's rarest and most threatened birds such as the Echo Parakeet the Mauritius Pink Pigeon and the Mauritius Kestrel. The birdwatcher may be lucky to catch glimpses of them but is more likely to spot the cuckoo shrike, flycatcher and Mauritius blackbird or the graceful white paille-en-queue (or tropic bird) swooping through the gorges. The paille-en-queue has been adapted as the Air Mauritius logo.

Back on the main Chamarel road, about 100m (328ft) after the third viewpoint, there is a small track on the right marked 'Peak of the Little Black River'. From here the walk to the highest point of the island at 828m (2,716ft) and back takes the best part of a day. The path, flanked on both sides by jungles of Chinese guava trees, narrows in parts to no more than a few feet. Now and again breaks in the thick jungle enable scintillating views across the Black River Gorge. This walk is best done in a group with a knowledgeable guide (see the Additional Information section at the end of this chapter for further details).

North-west from Le Pétrin are walking trails to **Mare Longue**

Reservoir looking like a tiny alpine lake. It was built as part of a hydro electric and irrigation scheme. From here there are more views of the Black River Gorge and the peak of the Little Black River (Piton de la Petite Rivière Noire). Beyond Mare Longue Reservoir a track leads to the **Tamarin Falls** or Sept Cascades where the River Tamarin tumbles over seven steps through a deep narrow tree-clad gorge.

Motorists can drive the 5km (3 miles) from Le Pétrin to Mare Longue by returning in the direction of Mare aux Vacoas and taking the marked road on the left. It is also possible to drive to Tamarin Falls by returning to La Marie via Mare aux Vacoas. Continue along the B64 to Glen Park and turn left on to the B65 to Henrietta. At the end of the village is a new bus station. Turn right and follow the tracks through sugar cane for about a kilometre until the road reaches the ridge of Tamarin Falls. The best views of the falls and the gorge sweeping out to sea are obtained from just after a small power house on the north-east edge.

Return to **Henrietta** where a visit may be made to the nurseries of Anthuriums and Orchids Limited. From Henrietta it is only a short distance to Curepipe and the motorway.

From Curepipe there is easy access to Le Val Nature Park (see Chapter 2, The East Coast) and by taking the motorway to Nouvelle France stunning views of the east coast and Mahebourg may be admired from the uplands. At the Nouvelle France roundabout take the first exit and turn left on to the B83, which is marked Le Val Nature Park. This road sweeps through tea plantations to the small village of Cluny. Turn left at the junction marked Bananes and follow the signs for Le Val. The road, bordered by travellers palms and delightful mauve indigenous orchids, winds uphill giving panoramic views across a deep valley to the Bambou Mountains. The area contains the biggest hydropower plant in Mauritius. The work necessitated the construction of a dam on the Grand River South East and the water is conveyed to a power station along a 3km (2 miles) tunnel across the Bambou Mountains.

Additional Information

Beau Bassin
Balfour Gardens
Open: daily from 6am-6pm.

Centre d'Excursion de Beau Bassin
38 Cite Vuillemin
☎ 454 0505 (through the secretary after 5pm)

A private group that welcomes overseas visitors on organised walks with experienced guides.

Curepipe
Botanical Gardens
Forestry Service (Conservator of
    Forests)

☎ 675 4966
Open: Monday to Friday 9am-4pm.
For full information on walks in
Black River area and for permits to
visit nature reserves.

Casino de Maurice
Boulevard Victoria
Open: 9pm-3am.
☎ 675 5021

Floreal
Adamas Duty Free Diamond Boutique
Mangalkan
☎ 686 5246, 686 5783
Open: 9am-4pm.

Henrietta
Anthurium Greenhouses
Anthurium & Orchids Limited
Vacoas
☎ 686 2915
Open: Monday to Friday 7am-
12noon and Saturday 7-11am.
There is a small entrance charge to
visit the shade houses.

Le Réduit (area)
Le Château du Réduit
Open: access to the grounds is
restricted if the château is being
used for official functions.
Otherwise open: Monday to Friday
9am-12noon

Moka (region)
Mahatma Gandhi Institute
☎ 454 7001
Open: Monday to Friday, 9am-4.30pm.

Eureka House
☎ 433 4951
Open: Monday to Friday 9am-4pm.

Phoenix
Mauritius Underwater Group
Clubhouse
Open: 8am-8pm Monday to
Saturday. Closing times on
Sundays and Bank Holidays
12noon. Tuesday night is club
night, closing at 11.30pm.

Quatre Bornes
Spes Boutique (Societe des Petites
Enterprises Specialisees)
7 Labourdonnais Avenue
☎ 425 7414
Open: Monday to Friday 9am-5pm.

Rose Hill
Craft-Aid (Mauritius) Co Ltd
Sir Edgar Laurent Street
☎ 464 2922
Open: Monday to Friday 8am-5pm.
Closed lunch 12noon-12.45pm,
weekends and public holidays.

Town Hall
☎ 454 3011
Open: Monday to Friday 9am-4.30pm
For details of events at the Plaza
Theatre, exhibitions at Max Moutia
Museum and Max Bouile Art Gallery
and sporting and cultural activities in
Rose Hill/Beau Bassin areas.

Tourist information and car hire
can be obtained from hotels and
travel agents.

7
RODRIGUES

Rodrigues, no more than a pinprick on even the most detailed of atlases, lies 653km (405 miles) east of Mauritius. To the north of Rodrigues is India, to the south is the Antarctic and eastwards the first landfall is western Australia 5,500km (3,410 miles) away. To contemplate a journey to one of the world's most remote islands requires stamina, determination and a sense of adventure. Having got there you will understand why Rodrigues is Mauritius' best kept secret. It is beautiful, simple and unpretentious, but do not expect five-star hotels, cocktails on the beach or disco dancing beneath the stars. A visit to Rodrigues is an experience in isolated island life and its appeal lies in its ruggedness and a feeling that you are going back in time.

Getting there needs a little planning. Air Mauritius ATR 42s make the flight five times a week but early booking is recommended. Visitors would be well advised to include the Rodrigues flight as a side trip when making their original booking to Mauritius and note that a 15kg baggage allowance applies. Some travel agents in Mauritius and abroad can organise inclusive tours with accommodation in simple guest houses.

The journey takes 90 minutes from SSR (Plaisance) Airport. Passengers landing at Plaine Corail Airport in the south are amazed at its diminutiveness. The terminal building, just manages to accommodate the fifty-odd crew and passengers from the Air Mauritius flight. There is no taxi service, but visitors should look out for a red and white Landrover. It belongs to Henri Meunier, Rodrigues' only tour operator-cum-taxi driver. In the unlikely event of it not being there, the aptly named airport bus, Supercopter, operates in conjunction with incoming flights and ferries passengers to the capital, Port Mathurin, 18km (11 miles) away.

130 • Visitor's Guide: Mauritius, Rodrigues & Reunion

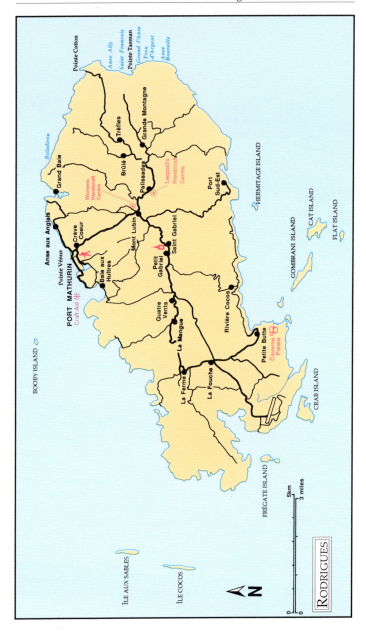

The alternative is to establish the sailing schedules of the cargo/passenger vessel, *Mauritius Pride* which are advertised in the local press. Built at a cost of 350 million rupees, it made its maiden voyage from Mauritius to Rodrigues in September 1989 and can accommodate 248 passengers in aircraft type seats and 12 first class passengers in six double cabins. First class passengers have access to a separate lounge, video screens, dining room and gymnasium. Tourist class passengers take meals in the cafeteria and there are toilet/shower facilities. The voyage time is 24 hours and for the present will be sailing approximately every 5 weeks. Tickets can be obtained from most local tour operators.

Shaped like a short plump fish measuring 18km (11 miles) in length and 8km (5 miles) in width, Rodrigues is completely surrounded by a lagoon almost twice the size of the island. Within the lagoon there are islets and atolls, some little more than sand banks, two of which are designated nature reserves. A hilly ridge extends from the south-west to the north-east from which descend a series of steep valleys to strips of coastal flatlands. South-east trade winds blow for most of the year tempering the hot tropical sun from November to April and rain and cyclones may develop during this period. Maximum temperatures vary from 23 °C (73 °F) in August to 32 °C (90 °F) in February. May to October are the coolest months and it can be chilly at night on high ground.

Rodrigues is the smallest and youngest island of the Mascarenes group reckoned to be about one and half million years old. Although early fifteenth-century Arab maps referred to it as *Dina Moraze*, its probable date of discovery was in 1528 when the Portuguese sailor, Diego Rodriguez, after whom the island is named, visited the island on his way home to Portugal from India.

The first landing was made by the Dutch in 1601 but they never settled. The first settlers were a group of nine Protestants led by a François Leguat, who fleeing religious persecution in France, set sail from Holland and arrived at Rodrigues in 1691. Their experiences are recorded in Leguat's book *Voyages and Adventures* which gives a remarkable insight into what the island was like before man's settlement. They lived in a healthy climate feasting on huge fat birds, palm cabbages, and seafood and drank fresh water and home-made wine. However, with no women to keep them company, the men became bored and abandoned the island 2 years later. They sailed for Dutch-occupied Mauritius only to be arrested as spies and were imprisoned on one of the small barren islands near Mahebourg. After several years in captivity they were released but only Leguat and one other made it back to Europe. A twenty-five cent stamp commemorating the settlement in Rodrigues was issued in 1987.

In 1725 a small party of men under Captain Boulanger of La Ressource was sent to colonise the island in the name of Louis XV of France. It was renamed Marianne after the king's fiancée, Marie-Anne Victoire, the Spanish infanta and daughter of Phillippe V of Spain. The colonisation ended in failure and the island was abandoned save for a few colonists and a small garrison who remained until Labourdonnais established a settlement in 1763. The garrison eventually withdrew in 1770.

During this period the island was ravaged of its thriving population of land and sea turtles. In spite of the official ban imposed by the French East India Company the plundering continued by pirates, corsairs and anybody else who saw the turtle as a convenient and transportable food. Meanwhile cyclones had ruined fresh provisions in the other Mascarene Islands and resulted in Labourdonnais authorising the transportation of some 10,000 turtles to the markets of Mauritius and Reunion.

There were eight island administrators between 1736 and 1809, amongst them a Philibert Marragon, but he angered the other settlers. They accused him of being an opportunist who far exceeded his authority by allowing the British to victual their ships at a time when the British were contemplating an attack on Mauritius.

Marragon's complacency caused General Decaen, the governor of Mauritius, to remove him from Rodrigues by offering him a posting in the Seychelles. When Marragon learned that they had been occupied by the British he returned to Rodrigues where he died in 1826 at the age of 76 years. His tombstone is hidden in the hills near Union behind Port Mathurin where he is buried with his wife.

After several reconnaisance trips, British troops under Lieutenant Colonel Keating took possession of Rodrigues in 1809 and the island was used as a base from which to launch an attack on Mauritius the following year. Three years later after British rule was established, the remaining forces withdrew to India.

In 1864, bones of the extinct soltaire, a bird similar to the Mauritian dodo, were found in the coral caves at Caverne Patate. A deeper search resulted in the discovery of more bones enabling experts to piece together a complete skeleton which is now displayed in the Museum of Zoology at Cambridge in England. In 1874 astrological observations of the Transit of Venus were made from Pointe Venus to the east of Port Mathurin. The British also established a police magistracy and examples of its colonial past can still be seen in the architecture of the administrative buildings around Port Mathurin.

Rodrigues went unnoticed due to its position in mid-ocean and were it not for the British Cable and Wireless Company laying a submarine telegraph cable in 1901 linking it with Mauritius it would have remained so. The cable completed the line of communication between Australia and Europe and Rodrigues became the chief booster station between the two continents. On 3 November 1970 the cable broke down, and with radio technology already established, it marked the end of an era in telecommunications.

The population grew very slowly during the nineteenth century and the official census of 1901 showed there were only 3,300 inhabitants. By 1934 the population trebled to cause sufficient concern over the availability of natural and physical resources. Emigration was seen as the solution and many Rodriguans settled in Reunion and Mauritius and farther afield in Australia. Some 1,000 Rodriguans served with the British Army during World War II but the population continued to grow even after the war primarily because of the lack of family planning services.

Rodrigues was administered by the British as an island dependancy of Mauritius until independence was achieved in 1968. It is now politically integrated and forms the tenth administrative district of Mauritius. Nevertheless its people remain fiercely independent aligning themselves more to the Creoles of African origin rather than those of its Indian-dominated sister island.

The islanders are of mixed origin and fall into two distinct groups: the descendants of the first European settlers and the descendants of African and Malagasy slaves who worked the sugar plantations in Mauritius. Ninety-five per cent of Rodriguans are Roman Catholics and churches are well attended by brightly dressed congregations. As in Mauritius, the official language is English although the lingua franca is Creole.

The government owns 90 per cent of the land which is leased to individual families on a 10-year renewable basis. Most of the islanders are fishermen and farmers who export most produce to Mauritius. While agriculture forms a substantial part of the economy, cultivable land is scarce due to overgrazing, frequent drought, cyclone and soil erosion. There is a very small domestic market for the manufacture of baskets and hats and the government is encouraging the development of handicraft workshops. Rodriguans rely almost entirely on the regular shipment of food, grains, consumer goods and petroleum products by sea transport although it is anticipated that reliance on Mauritius to supply these goods will be reduced by various government programmes to control soil erosion by terracing and afforestation, improving irrigation facilities and providing incentives to farmers. Tourism, although young, contributes a significant role in the economy.

A recommended map, published by the French Institut Geographique National, is available in Europe, Mauritius and Rodrigues. The official government map of Mauritius, published by the Ministry of Housing, Land and the Environment, also includes an insert of Rodrigues. In theory planning routes in Rodrigues is quite an easy task but quite different in practice. The arriving visitor cannot fail to notice the prevalence of four-wheel drive vehicles and a journey to virtually anywhere will demonstrate how essential they are. There is only one main road from Plaine Corail airport in the south to the capital Port Mathurin which gives access to roads and tracks to other parts of the island. Drinking water is of poor quality but bottled water is available at stores and restaurants. There are no private doctors or pharmacies but treatment may be obtained at any one of the three hospitals or local health centres. Visitors should bring their own medical supplies. There are very few shops beyond Port Mathurin and walkers should equip themselves with sturdy shoes and a sun hat and carry a supply of water and refreshments.

The abundance of reefs and wrecks in the waters around Rodrigues will appeal to divers who should bring all equipment, including cylinders. The waters are warm and a lycra suit should be sufficient. Henri Meunier is an ex-professional diver with 20 years experience whose intimate knowledge of the diving sites intrigues visiting divers. Excursions with him to explore the dozens of ship-wrecks, some dating back to the nineteenth century are memorable. Henri can arrange to have cylinders filled with air.

Henri Meunier operates from a blue and white painted office at Victoria Street, Port Mathurin. Excursions can be arranged in his Land Rover or he can be used as a taxi service. Travelling around the island independently is possible, but difficult, as bus services grind to a halt at 2pm so trips with Henri Meunier are highly recommended.

Whether flying or sailing to Rodrigues visitors are likely to end up at **Port Mathurin.** It was named after one of the first French settlers, Mathurin Brehinier, who with his family, were the only inhabitants of Port Mathurin. He waged relentless feuds with his closest neighbour, Philibert Marragon, who lived in the hills behind Port Mathurin. Today the atmosphere is more of a peaceful village than a capital town save for a few days each month when the cargo vessel arrives disgorging much needed supplies and creates excitement amongst the inhabitants on the quayside.

Looking inland from the red corrugated roofed boat-shaped jetty the town spreads in neat blocks with English street names. A war

A Rodriguan selling fierce home-bottled chilli and pumpkin

The solitaire is extinct except for its name above this basketware shop

136 • Visitor's Guide: Mauritius, Rodrigues & Reunion

memorial on the waterfront, erected by a former Island Commissioner, Maxime Labour, commemorates Rodriguan volunteers who fought in both World Wars.

To the right of the memorial is the fenced off area of the quayside and the customs sheds. A weekly market is held one block back in Fisherman Lane. Every Saturday the islanders trek from their isolated habitations in the hills carrying fierce home bottled chilli, pumpkin, coconut and tomatoes to sell in Port Mathurin. The market begins promptly at 6am and produce is sold out by 8am when the street resumes its former tranquil air. Most shops, no more than converted shacks with the nameplate of their owner and type of business on hand painted signs, are located in Jenner and Morrison Streets. Barclays Bank, on the corner of Jenner and Morrison Street, is particularly busy on the last Friday of the month when men and women collect their pay cheques in separate queues that often spill on to the pavement. The bank is open Monday to Friday 9.30am-2.30pm and 9.30-11.30am on Saturdays. Visa transactions involve sending telexes to Mauritius and can take about half an hour to complete. Other banks here are the Indian Ocean International Bank and Mauritius Commercial Bank.

Nearby a general store called Maxime Wong stocks everything from camera equipment, postcards and maps to essential foodstuffs while in Fisherman Lane, souvenirs of locally produced vacoas woven baskets spill out from a nameless store on to the street.

Continue along Morrison Street and three turnings on the right in Douglas Street is the bus station and some food stalls. Old wooden bungalows with corrugated roofs seem to have withstood the cyclones and contrast with the new air-conditioned offices of Air Mauritius, the State Commercial Bank and the Development Bank.

Many of the administrative buildings are to the left of the war memorial in an area enclosed by Jenner Street and the waterfront. A small entrance leads into the public park set around a hard tennis court. In the evening, islanders sit cross legged on the lawn and watch films on a communal television set.

On the perimeter of the gardens are the corrugated roofed buildings of the Police Station, Court House and Post Office. A magistrate comes from Mauritius once a month to preside over minor cases of drunkenness and petty theft. The proceedings are held in Creole and most defendants plead guilty. The District Administration Office, in nearby Jenner Street, is a colonial building dating back to 1879, from where permits must be obtained to visit the nature reserves of Île Cocos and Île aux Sables and the caves.

Opposite is the imposing residence of the Island Commissioner. A large, rambling colonial house built in 1873, it has lush gardens set behind high walls guarded by two World War II cannons.

Beyond the Island Commissioner's residence is the Ciel d'Ete Guest House. The three rooms have shared facilities and the windows face the afternoon sun. Meals are taken in a small dining room with a balcony. Two simple self-catering bungalows across Winston Churchill Bridge are also available at a slightly higher charge.

Beau Soleil Guest House, a few blocks back from Jenner Street in Victoria Street, is popular and reservations are strongly recommended. Breakfast is taken in the rooms or in the dining room with a view across the street. Evening meals for non-guests should be ordered by prior arrangement with the owner.

Ebony Restaurant in Jenner Street is open for lunch and evening meals. Managed by locals it caters for tourists and is expensive by Rodriguan standards but serves very good food and snacks and drinks in the adjacent bar. Of better value and in a homelier atmosphere try the Lagon Bleu next door to Henri Tours in Victoria Street. Complete with a 'mini-museum' consisting of a small display cabinet exhibiting finds of pieces of ships and coins recovered by diving enthusiasts there is also a makeshift library of books and magazines.

It is worthwhile calling at the little workshop called Craft-Aid in Victoria Street. This project is an extension of a similar project in Mauritius. Craft-Aid is a non-profit industry which provides creative and remunerative employment to people with disabilities. Visitors are warmly received and given a delightful guided tour of the workshop. Visitors are thanked for their interest with the presentation of a pressed flower card and are under no obligation to buy any of the unusual and reasonably priced souvenirs.

East along Jenner Street leads to the Winston Churchill Bridge across the Rivière Cascade. The road hugs the shore for most of the way, rising gently to a roundabout indicating inland for Mont Lubin, and straight ahead for English Bay (Anse aux Anglais).

Just past the roundabout a new harbour completed in 1991 was built to accommodate the *Mauritius Pride* and other ships. On the other side of the road are the red corrugated iron roofed huts of Port Mathurin Government School.

After the school a road inland indicates Queen Elizabeth Hospital at Crève Coeur. The road steepens with views across Port Mathurin and ends abruptly at the car park with access to the casualty department. The hospital, has a paediatric and maternity department.

Continue along the coast road for a short way to reach the Overseas Telephone Service office. It is open from 8am to 10pm. Calls are taken in small cubicles. The bungalow housing the OTS office used to be the administrative offices of the Cable and Wireless Company. A steep road climbs past the OTS office to the cyclone-proof hut of the Mauritius Broadcasting Corporation. Television was introduced to Rodrigues in 1987 but few households own a television set. Cassettes of news bulletins and items broadcast on Mauritian television are flown over and transmitted from the local office but this procedure can be delayed by cyclone or adverse weather conditions. Rodriguans raise a wry smile when news of cyclone warnings, for instance, arrive a few days after a cyclone has visited the island. In practice they find it easier to pick up French news broadcast from Reunion 720km (446 miles) away.

To the left of the hut is a huge wooden bungalow that used to be the staff quarters of the Cable and Wireless Company. The manager lived in a private bungalow further up the hill. It is believed that this building won prizes at the Ideal Home Exhibition at Earls Court, London in 1903. It was later dismantled into sections and shipped out to Rodrigues to be reconstructed as the manager's residence. The staff quarters and the manager's bungalow have been converted into the Pointe Venus Hotel. In spite of its basic facilities there are lovely ocean views from the spacious verandah where visitors can relax in comfortable whicker chairs in a truly colonial atmosphere.

A lovely coastal walk may be made to **Grand Baie** 5km (3 miles) eastwards from Port Mathurin. Continue past the Pointe Venus Hotel where a huge satellite dish installation, enabling telephone and telex communication, somehow looks out of place on the ruggedness of this coast. Cross a second bridge called Pont Soupirs to reach **Anse aux Anglais** (English Bay) where in 1761 a British squadron occupied the island without any opposition from the inhabitants. They were expecting reinforcements to arrive from India but none came and they withdrew a few months later. Just beyond the bridge there is a long stretch of golden beach with a picnic area fringed with filaos trees. The Filaos Guest House with six simply furnished rooms is set slightly back from the road. The local Rotary Club hold meetings in the attractive outdoor restaurant.

An asphalted road rises and falls to another stretch of beach called **Caverne Provert** with a grassy picnic area and more filao trees. Signs in English and French implore everyone to keep the beach clean and litter bins are in evidence. Clean and tiled public toilets built by the locals are at the far end of the beach.

A stiff uphill climb leads to a fairly flat area where acacia trees border the road. A path on the left leads to a headland which overlooks **Grand Baie.** This is an enormous sandy bottomed bay, isolated and rugged. Continue on a steep downhill trek to reach

Grand Baie but remember unless you can hitch a lift you will have to walk back up to Port Mathurin!

To the west of Port Mathurin is **Baie aux Huîtres** (Oyster Bay), an enormous deep bay surrounded by hills and deep forests of casuarinas. Many civil servants posted from Mauritius live here with their families along with the predominantly European descendants of the first French settlers. There are a few Chinese-run stores and the Venise discoteque which doubles as a restaurant and nightclub. On the other side of the bay, at Pointe la Guele, is the island's only prison.

A stiff uphill walk or drive from Port Mathurin to Mont Lubin, an inland village south of Port Mathurin, gives an idea of Rodriques' rugged landscape. Follow the road which climbs past the Meteorological Station. The radio transmitter in Mauritius is not powerful enough for the islanders to pick up signals so the station gives cyclone warning signs by hoisting coloured flags. A red flag indicates warning 1-3. Blue flags indicate the end of a cyclone.

Across the road from the Meteorological Station is **Pointe Canon** which gives panoramic views of Port Mathurin. On this grassy headland a black 2m (6ft) cannon looks out to sea. It was rescued from Mauritius and brought to Rodrigues where it was carefully

---

Rodriguan washday

140 • Visitor's Guide: Mauritius, Rodrigues & Reunion

painted and renovated. It stands near La Reine de Rodrigues, a white statue of the Virgin Mary. On the 1 May each year islanders walk up the steep hillsides from Port Mathurin to celebrate May Day.

The road continues to rise through thick forests of eucalyptus at **Solitude** and is bounded by deep valleys where small copses of jamrosa and mango trees provide food for the Rodrigues fruit bat. The road to Mont Lubin is quite well surfaced and is served by bus.

Mont Lubin is a shanty village, typical of many to be found on the island, with Post Office, hospital, social security office and a Womens Handicraft Centre. Friendly women sit in a cool dark hut where visitors are welcome to watch them tressing baskets woven from the local vacoas or buy any of the finished articles from the small display. At Mont Lubin the road splits. The right fork joins a good surfaced road to La Ferme and the airport at Plaine Corail.

The left fork is signposted for Grand Montagne and Pointe Cotton. Nearby Mont Limon is the highest point of the island at 393m (1,289ft). The route to Pointe Cotton will apeal to walkers. It is only accessible by walking or hitching a lift from Grand Montagne which is an excellent starting point to spend a day exploring the isolated and beautiful bays, coves and beaches of the east.

Just past the hospital at Mont Lubin a track on the left leads to Baladirou on the north coast which, from Port Mathurin, is only accessible on foot or by boat. From the main road heading east along the spine of the island there are sweeping coastal views Inland undulating fields of manioc, sweet potato and maize swathe the landscape before the road begins to drop at the hamlet of **Palissades.**

The huge wide-brimmed hats worn by so many Rodriguans and other items of basketwork can be bought at Leopold's Handicraft Centre situated in a small hut on the left hand side of the road at Palissades. Continue eastwards along the main road where there are panoramic views of the south, east and north coasts.

At **Grande Montagne** the road descends with views of ravines and verdant terraced hillsides of banana plantations, mango trees and the odd sugar cane field. When the cane is ripe in June it is not unusual to see Rodriguans marching along the roads sucking great sticks of sugar cane freshly cut from the fields.

Turn right less than 1km ($^1/_2$ mile) after Grand Montagne where a white arrow on a blue background indicates Pointe Cotton. The road is quite well surfaced and wide for about $3^1/_2$km (2 miles) before dipping slightly to **Trèfles** where four windmills have been installed to generate electricity. From here the landscape changes from the pockets of vegetation of the uplands to the ruggedness of the coast.

The road descends passing the isolated habitations of farmers and sweeps through acres of scrubby, rock-strewn pasture land. Black skinned locals gather the rocks and spend hours reducing them into manageable pieces with great sledgehammers. The stone is used for building and road construction.

Soon there are views of **Pointe Cotton** and the sea. The road sweeps through plots of onion fields and crosses a bridge to the Cotton Bay Hotel. Pointe Cotton has one of the loveliest sandy beaches of the island with its own lagoon. You can clamber over low coral cliffs or wander through thick forests of filaos trees. There are clean public toilets and the only other building on the beach is the weekend bungalow of the local curate. Objections were raised to the erection of a hotel fearing that nudity was incompatible with the religious tone of the island but the problem was overcome when the developers moved the proposed site further down the beach.

From Pointe Cotton it takes about 3 hours to walk westwards via Baladirou to Port Mathurin. South from Pointe Cotton allow an hour to continue to the superb beaches of Anse Ally, Saint Francois and Baie de l'Est. Swimmers should beware of strong currents particularly at Saint Francois where there is a channel between the reef. Protective shoes should be worn when wading through muddy waters to avoid contact with the laff or stonefish.

The walk continues inland from Baie de l'Est to Tasman and access, through protected forest land, to the marvellous coves and beaches of the most easterly point of Rodrigues. Looking out to sea it is hard to accept that the nearest land mass is the western coast of Australia, some 5,500km (3,410 miles) away.

The afforested area is fenced off to prevent access to grazing cattle who find the young shoots of plants and trees particularly wholesome. A watchman allows access to visitors and will look after vehicles of those brave and adventurous enough to have driven to this part of the island. The pathway is bounded by some protected species, including the indigenous ebony tree, and great forests of young casuarinas as well as clumps of acacia, the August flowering morouk and thickets of 'vielle fille'. The pathway rises uphill and runs parallel with the coast where it crosses a plateau of dead coral. From here massive white rollers pound the reef which in places is merely 100m (328ft) from the shore.

The paths rise and dip into the lovely coves of Grand L'Anse, Trou d'Argent, Anse Vacoas and Anse Bouteille. Trou d'Argent is excellent for swimming. In fact the whole coast as far as Port Sud-Est is one isolated paradise of beach, cove, bay and coral.

A day trip combining Port Sud-Est and the caves at Caverne Patate in the south can be made from Port Mathurin by taxi-jeep. Make for

Mont Lubin and turn right on to the main road which rises steadily along a high ridge forming the backbone of the island and the second highest point, Mont Malartic at 386m (1,266ft).

A surfaced road financed by foreign funds leads southwards to Port Sud-Est from Mont Lubin. About half way down, a monument commemorates the completion of the road in 1987. From here there are views over Port Sud-Est, with its little cyclone-proof houses thrown down on the hillsides like dominoes, and the little reef encircled coral atolls of Hermitage, Cat and Gombrani Islands. Gombrani Island, to the far west is a breeding station for Australian sheep. The road descends to Port Sud-Est crossing several causeways to Anse Morouk with its scrubby beach where Mauritian entrepreneurs dream of acquiring plots of land to build luxury hotels. In reality, it will be a long time before Rodrigues is able to cope with the demands of high class tourism. Trips to the islands can be arranged through Henri Meunier with fishermen from Port Sud-Est.

At Mont Lubin buses ply the route westwards to La Ferme. The **Church of Saint Gabriel**, merits a stop. It is one of the largest churches in the Port Louis diocese with a nave 50m (163ft) long by 19m (63ft) wide and an overall height of 12m (41ft). Work began in 1936 when men, women and children carried sand, coral, stone and cement from the coast to St Gabriel. The work took 15,000 days of voluntary labour, mostly on Sundays after mass, until the church was finally completed in 1939.

A few kilometres to the west at **Petit Gabriel** there are lovely views to the north of Oyster Bay. The road takes on a series of twists and turns until it reaches **Quatre Vents** where a bright crimson painted general store indicates the turning left for Rivière Cocos.

This road leads to the caves of **Caverne Patate** via the small habitations of Papaye and the Marechal Breeding Centre. At La Fouche take the left fork for Petite Butte. Look for a pink building housing the Community Centre on the left of the road and shortly afterwards turn right onto a dirt track. A little way down is a small shack which is the official watchmans' quarters. The permit to visit the caves must be shown to the watchman and in spite of his lack of English he volunteers to act as your guide.

The guide leads you on a magical, mystery tour of the caves. These inland coral caves lie some 18m (59ft) below sea level and are not for the faint-hearted or claustrophobic. The guide gives a dramatic account of how two Englishmen looking for the bones of the extinct solitaire were lost forever in the labyrinth. In fact this is a reference to the finding of the solitaire bones in 1864 by British naturalists. Much depends on yours and his imagination to discern the weirdly fashioned shapes of animals and monsters set amongst coral stalactites and stalagmites.

The caves have fascinated naturalists ever since their first official exploration in 1786 when bones believed to be those of the dodo were found by a French captain. In the 1860s deeper searches led to the discovery of more bones and comparisons with earlier findings proved they belonged to the solitaire.

The walk through the caves normally takes about half an hour but can take longer depending on the guide's enthusiasm. If you go with Henri Meunier he will introduce you to the guide and wait at the exit for you to emerge. Take your own torch.

Return to La Fouche and continue northwards to **La Ferme**, a large inland village which boasts a small football and athletic stadium where the Pope held mass when he visited Rodrigues in October 1989. In the main street there are several Chinese stores, a Post Office and Police Station and nearby a hospital and several schools. The village is only 110m (361ft) above the sea but to the north there are resplendent views of the little islands of Cocos and Sables.

A good place to stop for simple lunch is at John's Resto Bar, a delightful little restaurant in **La Mangue** village, just over 2km (1

Only small boats cross the lagoon to Île Cocos

144 • Visitor's Guide: Mauritius, Rodrigues & Reunion

mile) to the east of La Ferme. A large sign in French requests Rodriguan men to remove their hats on entering the premises as their headgear is quite often the size of Texan ten gallon hats.

ÎLE COCOS AND ÎLE AUX SABLES

Permits must be obtained from the District Administration Offices in Port Mathurin to visit Île Cocos and Île aux Sables. They are situated 11km (7 miles) from Port Mathurin and $3^1/_2$km (2 miles) from the western tip of Rodrigues. Cocos and Sables are narrow sand banks only 1.2km and 600m (1 mile and 1,968ft) respectively in length. They were transformed into nature reserves in 1980 following studies which showed that out of an estimated twelve species of indigenous birds only two were left. They are the last refuge of the noddy and the fairy tern which have virtually disappeared from Rodrigues.

Henri Meunier can arrange the permits if necessary. Otherwise first seek out a fisherman employed by the Fisheries Division and give him the permit. However independant attempts to find a fisherman employed by the Fisheries Division may be frustrating due to language difficulties. Times of departure depend on the tide as the voyage involves sailing across a shallow lagoon. On the way dozens of fish can be hooked and cooked on arrival at Cocos island by the government employed watchman. The Robinson Crusoe existence, with no running water, electricity, television or radio, is the ultimate experience in desert island living and is worth doing if only to walk barefoot along a mound of white floury sands rising from a turquoise clear lagoon and to hear the screaming chatter of a thousand birds from a forest of filao trees.

There are conditions: travel must be made in a boat provided by the Fisheries Division with no more than nine people, the lighting of fires, overnight camping and removal of flora and fauna are prohibited and access is restricted between 5pm and 7am.

Rodrigues is a forgotten island floating in the depths of a remote sea. It is also a welcome sight for a handful of yachtsmen and private adventurers who sail the Indian Ocean from Australia to Africa. It does not pretend to compete with the tourism of her sister island, Mauritius. Those who go there, go for its tranquillity and to experience a slice of isolated island life and to discover a friendly, curious and welcoming people. Things are as quiet at night as they are during the day, but if you take an evening stroll through Port Mathurin you will see the men congregating in drinking dens and probably you will be invited to join them. It is only then that you need little imagination to relate this modern life to the grog shops of the old days when pirates and corsairs 'rested' between raids and plied the garrison with rum in return for their silence. Outside the twentieth century is betrayed by crates of empties awaiting return to Mauritius while the younger generation cluster round the open-air communal television nearby and watch entranced at horror movies.

WILDLIFE

Sadly much of the original wildlife has disappeared. The solitaire, a large elegant goose-like bird, met the same fate as its cousin, the dodo, along with parrots, herons, owls, giant tortoises, geckos, sea turtles and dugongs. Of the diverse fauna, only the fruit bat and two bird species, the fody and the brush warbler remain. The only two heavily wooded areas where bat colonies are found are the valleys of Cascade Pigeon and Solitude although there are some isolated areas of natural forest. To spot the bat colonies take the main road behind Port Mathurin to the top of the island at Mont Lubin where in the early evening they fly over to their feeding area and feast on the fruit of the mango tree and a variety of leaves and flowers. Reafforestation of the island is a priority with the Forestry Department who, by careful nurturing, hope that some of the wildlife will survive and re-establish stable populations.

There are no poisonous snakes in Rodrigues — only some uncommonly large spiders who festoon their webs across the tops of electric cable-carrying pylons, and 6 inch long centipedes which, if disturbed, can inflict a painful sting.

Additional Information

Mont Lubin
Womens Handicraft Centre
Open: Monday to Friday 8am-2pm.

Palissades
Leopold's Handicraft Centre
Open: Monday to Friday 8am-2pm.

Port Mathurin
District Administration Office
Open: Monday to Friday 9am-4pm for permits to visit Île Cocos and Île aux Sables. A fee must be paid to the official cashier who will issue a receipt. Permits to visit the caves at Caverne Patate are free.

Craft Aid
Open: Monday to Friday 8am-3pm.

Useful Address

Henri Tours
Henri Meunier
Victoria Street
Port Mathurin
☎ 8311 635
Further information may be obtained from the Mauritius Government Tourist Offices on accommodation (see Fact File and other chapters for details).

8
REUNION

Reunion is the largest of the Mascarene Islands lying only 165km (102 miles) to the south-west of Mauritius. Regular daily flights from SSR (Plaisance) Airport connect with Reunion and the journey takes a mere half hour leaving barely enough time to finish the in-flight complimentary drink before landing at Gillot International Airport.

As an overseas department administered by France it is not surprising that the majority of visitors are French. Sadly, English-speaking tourists staying in Mauritius tend to overlook the ease and accessibility of Reunion and even fewer consider turning their Indian Ocean holiday into a two-centre stay.

Reunion lies very much in the shadow of Mauritius, but possesses a certain rugged beauty which is reflected in a powerful interior of mysterious mountains, peaks, gorges, rivers and forests. She offers the freedom to explore a fascinating and still active volcano that sits huffing and puffing like a grand old lady with a furious temper and three extinct craters, known as 'cirques', which are peppered with isolated villages.

The island has its share of beaches although visitors who have spent a holiday in Mauritius may well be disappointed not to find any of such comparable splendour in Reunion. Only 30 of its 207km (19 and 128 miles respectively) coastline are devoted to beach with a sprinkling of coral reef. Consequently the beaches get crowded especially at the weekend and the Reunionese either escape to Mauritius for an extended sun, sea and sand holiday or to Rodrigues for its charming simplicity. Mauritians, on the other hand, are drawn to Reunion's awe-inspiring vistas of mountains and craters and its active volcano whose eruptions are still altering the shape of the island. Reunion does not promise the idyllic beaches of Mauritius

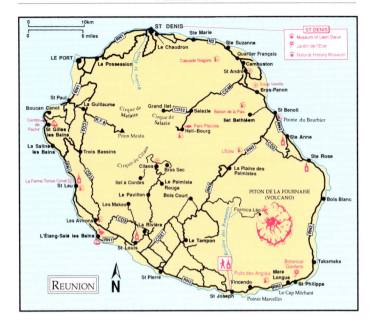

but its tourism infrastructure caters for all visitors from the most sophisticated and demanding to the more budget-conscious and adventurous traveller enabling all to experience yet another slice of Mascarene Island life in an unmistakably French atmosphere.

Reunion shares a similar history with the other Mascarene Islands and features prominently in the great maritime struggle between the European powers for supremacy in the Indian Ocean. Charted as *Dina Morgabin* by the Arabs, *Santa Apollina* by the Portuguese, it was renamed *Mascarin* and then *Bourbon* by the French in 1642 after Governor Pronis of the infant French East India Company was ordered by the king of France to establish a presence in the Indian Ocean. Mauritius with its fine harbour would have been perfect but its occupation by the Dutch forced him to sail southwards and establish a settlement at Fort Dauphin in Madagascar.

Life in Madagascar was intolerably hard and the men under Pronis soon mutinied against him. He reacted by deporting a dozen ringleaders to uninhabited *Bourbon* in 1646 with a handful of Malagasy women for company. They were abandoned on the beach and left to lead a frugal life planting tobacco and melons. Two years later Etienne de Flacourt arrived in Madagascar to investigate the mutiny

148 • Visitor's Guide: Mauritius, Rodrigues & Reunion

and to reorganise the company's affairs. He ordered the release of the mutineers only to replace them in 1654 with another seven mutinous Frenchmen and a batch of dissidents from Malagasy. Conditions in Madagascar grew steadily worse and settlers stole boats and slipped away to endure the difficult 800km (496 miles) voyage to Bourbon. Amongst them were Louis Payen, his French servant and ten Malagasy men and women who arrived in 1662 where they learnt that the mutineers had fled to India. They became the islands first settlers.

The government could not entice enough people from France to start a new life so far from home in spite of them dubbing the island 'Eden'. The new settlers found the conditions not far short of hell and those that could left at the earliest opportunity. The governors then encouraged European pirates from Madagascar to drift to *Bourbon* where it was hoped they would live peacefully alongside the inhabitants. Some did, but many took advantage of the opportunity to recruit like-minded individuals and in no time at all organised raiding parties on vessels of the East India Companies.

Coffee was introduced in 1715 and sugar was developed as a crop in the first half of the nineteenth century bringing with it the need to import slaves from Madagascar and Africa. Some of them escaped and became known as *marrons* or the runaways. During this period the slave population rose from about 300 to 60,000 in 1848 when slavery was abolished.

Settlers left the island for Mauritius in 1721. The exodus resulted in severe damage to *Bourbon's* economy and was compounded in 1735 when the governor of Mascarene Islands, Mahé de Labourdonnais, transferred the headquarters of the French East India Company to Mauritius.

With privateering threatening trade in the Indian Ocean throughout the latter half of the eighteenth century, the British decided to take *Bourbon*. Its lack of defence made it an easy capture for the British who then took Rodrigues and finally Mauritius in 1810. By the Treaty of Paris in 1814 *Bourbon* became known as Reunion and was returned to the French. From then on successive governors did their best to put the island back on an economic footing.

The island suffered from manpower problems following the abolition of slavery in 1848 and an Anglo-French agreement allowed Reunion to import Indian immigrants on similar terms to Mauritius. However conditions were so bad that many Indians returned to their homelands when their contracts finished.

The island prospered due to the development of the sugar industry but fell into severe economic decline which lasted until after World War I when some 14,000 soldiers were sent to France. On 19

March 1946 Reunion became a French Overseas Department.

The island can be described as 'the France of the Indian Ocean' — at a price. With the French franc as the currency prices tend to be 30 per cent more than in France. Administered by a prefect delegated from Paris, the island consists of four arrondissements and a total of twenty-four 'communes' or districts. The population consists of a delightful melange of European, Malagasy, Indians and Chinese whose lingua franca is Creole although French is the official language. English is rarely spoken other than by those involved in tourism and commerce. The capital, St Denis is reminiscent of Paris with its boulevards, smart shops, outdoor cafés and restaurants while the coast road from the airport to St Denis, and beyond to the west, is a carbon copy of the busy bustling corniche of the riviera resort. The majority of the population is Roman Catholic reflected by the number of towns which bear the name of saints but the truth is that most have been named after famous sons of the island.

Entirely volcanic in origin, Reunion is three million years old and covers an area of 2,510sq km (965sq miles). It consists of two mountain masses. The oldest, in the north-west, covers two thirds of the total area and rises to form the Piton des Neiges at 3,096m (10,155ft) the highest peak of the Mascarene Islands. The remaining third of the island is of more recent origin and culminates in the Piton de la Fournaise at 2,613m (8,571ft), a still active volcano. Between these two mountain masses lies a high plain of an average altitude of 1,520m (4,986ft). To the north of this plain and with the Piton des Neiges at its centre three huge caldera-like valleys or 'cirques' radiate north, east and south-west. The mountains dip sharply to a narrow coastal plain with small stretches of beach mainly in the west.

Reunion boasts a tropical climate with two seasons: the hot season from December to April and the cool season between May and November. On the coast the temperature varies between 18°C (64°F) and 31°C (88°F). Inland this can drop to between 4°C (39°F) and 25°C (77°F) depending on altitude and season. At heights approaching 2,000m (6,560ft) temperatures may drop to below freezing.

The popular beaches are at St Gilles les Bains and Boucan Canot on the west coast. Sea temperatures vary between 28°C (82°F) in November to May and 24°C (75°F) June to October. Traditionally people take to the roads on Sundays when beaches get very crowded. However Reunion's main tourist attraction are the mountains which dominate the interior.

Exploring the island independently is best done by car. Major international car rental companies such as Avis, Hertz and Europcar operate from desks at Gillot Airport. An international driving licence

Isolated villages pepper the cirques

A Reunionese family

is required and drivers should be over 22 years of age. The following touring routes are designed for visitors arriving from Mauritius who would on average spend about a week on the island. A recommended map is the *Carte Touristique No 512* published by Institut Geographique National available in Europe, Reunion and Mauritius. There is an excellent asphalted road network with clear road signs and driving is on the right. Allow plenty of time and caution to complete these routes as the roads, particularly in the interior, twist and turn and narrow considerably and, save for the villages and towns, are unlit at night. Arrange any overnight mountain accommodation in advance and if planning to return to your starting point allow plenty of time for the return trip. Fuel stations are plentiful but most are closed on Sundays.

Piton de la Fournaise Volcano

The following touring route starts from St Benoit although if staying in the south-west it is possible to reverse the itinerary from St Pierre via Le Tampon.

St Benoit is 45km (28 miles) from St Denis and lies on the north-east coast. From here take the RN3 for Plaine des Palmistes which is clearly signposted. The road is straight and ascends gradually through fields of sugar cane for about 7km (4 miles) until it forms a hairpin bend to the right at Chemin de Ceinture and continues in a series of switchbacks to **L'Echo** (683m, 2,240ft) where there are lovely views of St Benoit and the ocean. From L'Echo the road climbs to an altitude of 1,100m (3,608ft) to La Plaine des Palmistes. Continue through another series of switchbacks to **Col de Bellevue** (1,606m, 5,268ft) where good parking facilities enable even better views of countryside sweeping down to the coast. At Le Vingt Septième, just after the Auberge du Volcan, take the RF5 on the left to reach the volcano. This is clearly signposted Nez de Bouef at 9km (6 miles) and the Route Touristique du Volcan.

From here the road winds uphill and is well signposted. At **Nez de Boeuf** (2,126m, 6,973ft), there are superb views of the gorge of the Rivière du Rempart. The river, appearing like a pencil line from these heights, flows southwards to St Joseph. The RF5 continues past Piton Textor (2,164m, 7,100ft) where signs indicate 4km (2 miles) to Plaine des Sables. An information board describing the surrounding mountains overlooks the Plaine des Sables with its extraordinary flat landscape. The road then descends to Plaine des Sables. Notice how the vegetation has changed from lush forestland to sparse bushes of gorse, heather and lichen sprouting from blackish red earth.

The **Pas de Bellecombe** is only 3km (2 miles) away. A tourist footpath allows access into the enclosure called Enclos Fouque. This is a horseshoe-shaped area surrounding the active Piton de la Fournaise volcano which dominates the south-east and overlooks the ocean. The summit has two craters: the highest, Le Bory, has been inactive since 1791 while the Dolomieu regularly erupts confining the lava within the Enclos. Occasionally the lava flows down towards the sea. The last major eruption occured in March 1986.

There are parking facilities and a mountain *gîte* at Pas de Bellecombe. Hot drinks can be bought at the *gîte* and overnight accommodation arranged provided at least 24 hours notice is given. It is an excellent base from which to explore the volcano. About 3 to 4 hours should be allowed to complete the walk which is best done early in the day as mist and cloud are common at these altitudes (2,300m, 7,544ft). Warm and waterproof clothing is recommended and walkers are strongly advised to keep to the marked paths.

Motorists can drive the to **Formica Léo** where they can leave their vehicles and continue along a footpath to the Chapelle Rosemont, a curious hollow volcanic mound which looks like a small cathedral complete with a door and window. Shortly afterwards the path splits into two. The right fork climbs for 2km (1 mile) before reaching the 200m (656ft) wide Bory crater. The left fork which is less arduous skirts the other side of the volcano for 2km (1 mile) and allows wonderful views of the 900m (2,952ft) active crater of the Dolomieu.

There are several waymarked paths in the Pas de Bellecombe area. One of the loveliest starts from Plaine des Sables via Nez de Coupe, where there are fine views of the volcano. The path then descends through verdant forestland to Puits de Tremblet on the east coast. At least 9 hours should be allowed to complete the 25km ($15^1/_2$ mile) hike. Further information on these and other walks can be obtained from the tourist office or the Maison de la Montagne in St Denis (see the Additional Information section at the end of this chapter).

Motorists should retrace the route along RF5 to Vingt Septième on the RN3 and take the left fork to Le Tampon passing through **Plaine des Cafres**. Once the hideout of runaway slaves, it is a good stop for refreshment and accommodation. The immense area of the Plaine des Cafres is bounded by two rivers, the Rivière des Remparts to the east and the Bras-de-la-Plaine to the west.

Either continue along the N3 to Le Tampon or take the D36 eastwards for a longer and more interesting route visiting Notre Dame de la Paix and Le Grand Tampon. An alternative side trip can be made from Plaine des Cafres to **Bois Court** 4km (2 miles) north on the D70 where there is a viewpoint overlooking Grand Bassin and the remparts at the south-eastern edge of the Cilaos cirque.

The tortuous N3 descends to **Le Tampon**, named after the Malagasy word *tampony* which means a peak. The area thrives on cattle breeding and sugar cane production and fields of geranium are cultivated for the extraction of essential oils for use in the perfumery industry. The town has several good pensions, hotels and restaurants making it an ideal base from which to explore the volcano.

It is 8$^1/_2$km (5 miles) by good motorway to the town of St Pierre on the south coast.

The Cirques

The three main cirques or craters are defunct volcanoes and are areas of scenic beauty situated in a clover like pattern in the centre of the island. Each cirque is an enormous valley of forest and mountain interspersed with farmland and isolated villages. Access to each is gained by taking roads inland from the main coast roads (RN1 or RN2). These roads lead only to the craters so it is not possible to continue a journey onwards or to visit another crater by car. However waymarked routes for walkers link one cirque with the other. The itinerary for motorists visiting the three cirques is shown by naming the starting points on the coast such as St André to Salazie, St Louis to Cilaos and St Paul to Mafatte via Maïdo.

St André to Salazie

The drive to Salazie is perhaps the easiest of all to complete and takes about 2 hours from St André. Follow the RN2 out of St André about 2km (1 mile) where a bridge crosses the Rivière du Mat. Do not cross the bridge but take the CD48 keeping right for Salazie. This road bordered by banana trees runs parallel with the river on the left and meanders gently uphill affording breathtaking views of waterfalls, tree-clad gorges and luxuriant vegetation. After about 7km (4 miles) it swings sharply left at another bridge crossing the Rivière du Mat which is now on the right. The bridge, Pont d'Escalier, marks the entrance to the cirque of Salazie and is surrounded by the soaring peaks of La Roche Ecrite (2,277m, 7,469ft) in the west and the Piton des Neiges (3,070m, 10,070ft) in the south. The road continues for another 7km (4 miles) before reaching the village of Salazie.

Salazie comes from the Malagasy word *salazane* which means a stake or post and is believed to have been named after the three peaks of the Le Gros Morne which stand like sentry posts at the far southwestern corner of the cirque. Salazie is the most verdant of all the cirques. Its inhabitants grow water cress, tobacco, coffee beans,

The Mafatte cirque can only be reached on foot or by helicopter

The Dolomieu crater at Piton de la Fournaise

apples, sugar cane and an abundance of *chou chou*, a lime green pear-shaped vegetable similar in taste to zucchini. The *chou chou* is of such great economic importance that each year in May the harvest is celebrated by the villagers at the three day carnival-like Festival of the Chou Chou. Inhabited by runaway slaves and then by white French settlers from the coast from 1830, Salazie today is a bustling community with shops, post office, banks, hotels, a youth hostel and numerous private accommodations.

One kilometre ($^1/_2$ mile) beyond Salazie and still on the CD48 the spectacular waterfalls of **Voile de la Mariée** (Brides Veil) cascade into the Rivière du Mat. At this junction, to the right, the CD52 snakes for 34km (21 miles) through the heart of the cirque to the hamlet of Grand Ilet which is overshadowed by the sky-prodding peak of La Roche Ecrite. Forest walks can be started at Belier, 3km (2 miles) on from Grand Ilet, where it is possible to park the car and take waymarked paths via the GR1 to the Mafatte and Cilaos cirques.

Beyond the waterfalls back on the CD48 and continuing to Hell-Bourg several viewpoints overlook Mare a Poule d'Eau with its calm waters set against a background of tamarin forest.

The discovery of medicinal springs bubbling up from the floor of the crater at what is now **Hell-Bourg** in 1831 drew the sick to Salazie. The springs were renowned for their healing properties for over a century until they were destroyed by a landslide following a cyclone in 1948. The remains can be seen from the heights of the Hotel des Salazes en route to Ilet a Vidot. Hell-Bourg, named after Governor De Hell who promoted agriculture in the region, boasts picturesque creole houses, several comfortable hotels and good restaurants. Lovely shaded picnic areas and ample parking make it a popular weekend retreat for locals and is a good starting point for walks from the GR1. Well marked signs indicate the Parc Piscicole D'Hell-Bourg (Freshwater Trout Farm) near the Relais des Cimes Hotel. The farm is set in verdant forestland and entrance is free. Bait and line are provided for visitors and a charge is made for any trout that are caught. There is a small snack bar and restaurant where trout can be cooked to order.

If not planning to stay overnight in Salazie allow sufficient daylight hours for the return trip on the steep unlit road.

St Louis to Cilaos

There is little to attract the visitor in the town of St Louis other than it being a convenient starting point for Cilaos. Cilaos, from the Malagasy *tsy laosana*, means the place one never leaves although some historians maintain it was named in memory of a marron leader Tsiloas who launched attacks on white settlers from the safety of its mountains. It is dominated by the Piton des Neiges and ever since thermal springs were discovered in 1819 by a goat hunter. It has been a popular resort for the infirm who in former times were ferried there by sedan or palanquins. Today it boasts a modern thermal and healing centre with an extensive range of treatments and is an excellent starting point for hikes and walks.

From St Louis, take the RN5 which twists its way along 38km (24 miles) to the cirque. For the first 6km (4 miles) it rises gently through the picturesque village of **La Rivière** with its gaily painted Creole houses and lush gardens. Drive cautiously through the village as there are deep gulleys on either side of the road. Beyond La Rivière the road narrows to the width of one vehicle until it runs parallel with the Bras de Cilaos river on the right. It is then a steady uphill climb which at each twist of the road opens up new vistas of cloud-capped mountains and isolated villages dotted in deep ravines.

The road descends through a series of switchbacks until crossing a bridge over the Bras de Cilaos river. This point, **Le Pavillion**, marks the entrance of the cirque where early travellers were transported by palanquin to Cilaos. Today it is a delightful watering hole called Le Relais du Pavillion and offers accommodation amidst superb views of soaring vegetation-clothed mountains.

Half way between La Pavillion and Cilaos, a detour along the CD240 on the right leads to the pretty hamlet of **Le Palmiste Rouge** 2km (1 mile) away. This area is famous for its mandarins, maize, bananas and watercress.

Many of **Cilaos** inhabitants are descendants of the eighteenth-century sttlers from Normandy and Brittany. They live in hamlets within the cirque and are involved in tourism, agriculture and the three long established activities of embroidery, wine making and lentil production for which Cilaos is famous. The town, at 1,220m (4,002ft), is reminiscent of the French alpine resort of Chamonix and is in fact twinned with it.

An embroidery workshop was founded in 1953 and is run by nuns who teach their skills to young girls. Visits can be arranged through the tourist office next door or displays admired at the Maison de la Broderie. Intricately hand-embroidered items can be bought from street stalls in Cilaos.

The Grand Hotel Des Thermes built in 1938 dominates the town. For many years the sick used it as a base to bathe in the thermal springs but a cyclone in 1948 destroyed the area.

However, with the opening of the Thermal Establishment of

Irenee-Accot in 1987, Cilaos has become one of the highlights of any stay on Reunion. Here weary walkers can indulge themselves in a full range of beauty and health treatments in saunas, massage rooms, gymnasia and jacuzzi and sufferers of digestive disorders, rheumatism and arthritis can be treated to the healing properties of the thermal waters under the supervision of medically qualified staff. A full tariff of treatment is available in the foyer.

The road splits in front of the Hotel des Thermes. For an exhilarating walk turn left at the hotel and take the road which runs parallel with the GR1 towards the Mafatte cirque in the north-west. Alternatively the isolated hamlet of **Ilet à Cordes**, 11km (7 miles) from Cilaos, may be reached by turning southwards after crossing the Bras Rouge river.

To the right of the hotel the road winds and climbs for 7km (4 miles) passing through a wonderful forest of tall cryptomeria trees. From here it is possible to park vehicles and wander through waymarked forest paths towards Piton des Neiges. Otherwise continue to the village of **Bras Sec**, noted for its vineyards and peache and delightful gardens of hydrangea, rose and bougainvillea. In makeshift cellars and workshops, the inhabitants produce the distinctively sweet red and white wines of Cilaos which can be tasted and bought in litre bottles.

There are good restaurants and reasonably priced bed and breakfast accommodation in Cilaos. If planning the stay overnight to walk the good 4 hours to Piton des Neiges the next morning, it is best to reserve accommodation at the *gîte* at Caverne Dufour, through the tourist office in St Denis or at the Maison de la Montagne at Cilaos.

St Paul to Mafatte via Maïdo

This cirque is the least populated of all. The road from St Paul finishes at Maïdo situated on the rim of the Mafatte cirque at 2,190m (7,183ft) and thereafter the only way of getting around is on foot.

Allow at least 2 hours to complete the winding 25km ($15^1/_2$ mile) drive from St Paul leaving early in the morning before cloud and mist have had a chance to obscure what must be some of the loveliest mountain scenery in the Mascarenes. Leave St Paul via the main RN1 in the direction of St Gilles-les-Bains and turn left on to the CD6 which is signposted to Guillaume, passing through La Renaissance. Here turn left on to the CD8 and after about $2^1/_2$km ($1^1/_2$ miles) turn left on to the CD4. After $1^1/_2$km (1 mile) take the CD7 on the right to Guillaume. After Guillaume at a T-junction turn left on to the CD3. After 1km ($^1/_2$ mile) turn right on to the RF8. This well asphalted road leads directly to Maïdo.

The road ascends into the foothills of the Grand Benare mountains at Petit France where sugar cane provides an expanse of undulating greenery. These are followed by great fields of geranium especially cultivated for their essential oils. Higher up at 1,200 to 1,500m (3,936 to 4,920ft) forests of tamarin, oak, beech and silver birch clothe the heights of the mountains before reaching Maïdo.

At **Maïdo** there are breathtaking views across the highest peaks of the island. Looking from left to right is La Roche Ecrite (2,277m, 7,469ft), Le Cimendef (2,226m, 7,301ft) and Le Morne du Fourche (2,195m, 7,200ft) which separate the Salazie and Mafatte cirques. The peaks of Le Gros Morne (2,991m, 9,810ft) and the Piton des Neiges (3,070m, 10,070ft) rise from the Salazes range of mountains marking the centre of the three cirques. To the south Le Col du Tabit (2,083m, 6,832ft) and the peak of Grand-Benare (2,896m, 9,499ft) divides Mafatte and Cilaos cirques providing a spectacular panorama.

Many excellent walks can be started from Maïdo and the five *gîtes* within the cirque situated at La Nouvelle, Grand-Place, Marla, Aurere and Roche Plate provide the rambler with accommodation and refreshment. Reservations should be made in advance at La Maison de la Montagne in St Denis.

WALKING ITINERARY OF THE THREE CIRQUES

No visit to Reunion would be complete without spending at least one night in the mountains if only to wake at sunrise and gaze upon deep and mysterious valleys clothed in magnificent forests. The air is clear and sharp and rouses even the weariest to explore and experience a walker's paradise of soaring spectacular peaks.

Overnight hotel or guest house accommodation is available in Salazie and Cilaos. Both are comfortable bases from which to explore the hundreds of kilometres of the Grand Randonnée (GRR1) which connect the plains, ravines and escarpments of the three great cirques. The paths are maintained by the Organisation National des Forêts (Forestry Department) and are clearly marked with horizontal red and black stripes. Distances and altitudes of destinations are clearly shown along with the approximate time it takes to get there.

Four days should be allowed to complete the 85km (53 miles) walk starting from Cilaos via Marla, La Nouvelle, Col de Fourche and finishing at Bélier in the Salazie cirque. Walkers are advised to take provisions of food and water, a light waterproof, sturdy walking shoes, torch and warm clothing. There are ten mountain *gites* strategically located in or around the cirques and all provide shelter and food. Reservations should be made through the *gîtes* La Maison de la Montagne in St Denis. A shorter half day walk can also be made to La Roche Ecrite midway between Mafatte and Salazie cirques starting from St Denis or a full day's walk to Le Dimitile on the south-east flank of Cilaos starting from Entre Deux.

HELICOPTER TOURS

For those with limited time, a helicopter tour is the easiest and most satisfying way of seeing the island. Reservations can be made through hotels or direct with the companies (see Additional Information). The experience is unforgettable as the pilots fly in and out of deep ravines and hover precariously over isolated hamlets. Amongst the tours offered is a visit to the least accessible Mafatte cirque where lunch is provided and a leisurely opportunity is given to explore the area before returning to base.

ISLAND TOUR

The mountainous nature of Reunion provides only a narrow coastal plain around the island upon which the large towns are situated. Although there is a complex network of good roads linking with the interior, there is but one main and well asphalted road which connects with the towns, providing fast and easy access around the island. A tour of the island can be made in a day but an early start is advised as there is much to see. It is also fortunate for the motorist that there are only two identifications for the coastal road: in the east from St Denis to St Pierre it is known as the RN2 and in the west from St Denis to St Pierre it is the RN1. The following tour runs in a clockwise direction from St Denis.

ST DENIS TO STE ROSE (61KM, 38MILES)

A good fast motorway (RN2) from St Denis links with Gillot Airport 10km (6 miles) away. Beyond the airport at 2km (1 mile) lies the busy town of **Ste Marie**. It is an important sugar cane area and the equable climate provides for the cultivation of tropical fruits such as mango and lychees. The RN2 sweeps through the centre of the town with the 1860s built French colonial style Mairie to the left.

The road continues eastwards for 6km (4 miles) to **Ste Suzanne** which takes its name from the river. Hand made bamboo bird cages and baskets can be found here although most inhabitants are employed in sugar, maize and vanilla production.

The lovely nineteenth-century built Church of Ste Suzanne is in the centre of the town near the bus station. In front of the church, partially hidden by an enormous flamboyant tree, is a statue of Poilu, the great veteran of World War I and a memorial to the men of Ste Suzanne who lost their lives in the war.

Cascade Niagara, a mini version of the Niagara Falls, makes an interesting detour from Ste Suzanne. The potholed road is well signposted from Ste Suzanne and traverses sugar cane fields until it passes a large white colonial house. Take the first junction on the right immediately after the house and continue to the end where the falls cascade into a delightful lake and flow into the Rivière Ste Suzanne. At weekends brave children dive into the lake from the black basalt rocks to the horror and amusement of day trippers.

Retrace the route back to town and follow the RN2 southwards crossing the Riviére Ste Suzanne. The road veers inland for 3km (2 miles) to **Quartier Français** where Reunion's first settlers arrived in 1646 as mutineers banished from Fort Dauphin in Madagascar. A detour may be made on the D47 to **Cambuston** and the coastal environs of St André. Here are the remains of the Church of Champ-Borne which was destroyed during the French Revolution. Otherwise remain on the RN2 to reach the town of St André which is a good starting point to reach the Salazie cirque.

St André is an important sugar cane centre. Following the abolition of slavery in 1848, indentured labourers were imported from India to work in the sugar cane fields. Many returned to India at the conclusion of their contract but those that settled continued to practise the Hindu religion and soon built their own temples. Today the Tamil Hindu Indians form about 25 per cent of the population and many live in St André where they are employed in agricultural activities. There are two Tamil temples in St André, the Shiva Soupramanual just before arriving in the town and the Karly Temple situated in the centre. Shoes should be removed if entering the temples. As in Mauritius, the Cavadee Festival is celebrated here. Details of dates can be obtained from the tourist office.

The RN2 continues from St André and cuts back towards the coast for 6km (4 miles) to the former coffee growing area of **Bras-Panon**. Sugar cane and vanilla are the principle crop of this small community.

Reunion is one of the world's leading producers of vanilla and the 1968 built Coop Vanille, just outside the town en route to St Benoit, is worth visiting. Vanilla is the only member of the orchid family that yields a product of commercial importance. In 1819 cuttings were brought to the island from Central America but experiments at natural pollination repeatedly failed. Then in 1841 a young slave called Edmund Albius discovered that the flowers could be pollinated by grafting. Guided tours of the factory and grounds showing the various stages of vanilla production are available from the reception and include the showing of a video film. All products made in the factory, including delicately hand-woven baskets of vanilla pods, can be purchased at the well stocked tourist office next door to the reception.

A detour may be made to **Bassin de la Paix** where its white waterfalls are at their most beautiful at sunrise. To get there take the road inland from the RN2 immediately after crossing the Rivière des Roches at Bras-Panon. The road, bounded by sugar cane to the left and river to the right, is asphalted for about 5km (3 miles) until it degenerates into a rough path across a bridge where there is a house. A pathway at the rear of the house leads to the waterfalls via a set of steps for which about 20 minutes should be allowed to negotiate their descent into the waterfalls.

Back on the RN2 lovely views may be admired from the grassy headland at **Pointe du Bourbier** where the fury of the Indian Ocean beats relentlessly on the black volcanic beaches of the eastern coast. Inland from this point the D53 rises gently through sugar cane fields for 5km (3 miles) to **Ilet Bethléem**. A half hour's walk along a footpath leads to the tiny chapel of the same name with delightful views of the tranquil waters of the Rivière des Marsouins.

St Benoit is the next main town from Bras-Panon lying in a former coffee growing area overlooking more black beaches. The centre of town is dominated by the Town Hall and memorial commemorating World War I and the colonial style Church of St Benoit with its black basalt columns. With plenty of shops, hotels, restaurants and covered market it is conveniently located for an excursion to the volcano.

The Baroque style Church of Ste Anne lies 5km (3 miles) to the south on the RN2 just before reaching the town of **Ste Anne**. Classed as a historic monument the church featured in the production of Francois Truffaut's film *The Sirene of the Mississipi*. The Baroque façade is the work of a Roman Catholic priest, Father Domemberger, who came to the town in 1922. He spent many years renovating the church until his death in 1948. His body is buried inside the chapel with its fine fresco work is dedicated to Ste Theresa. Next door Maison d'Artisanat sells handicrafts, souvenirs, postcards and essential oils.

At Ste Anne the road leaves the coast and winds a little way into the foothills of the volcano crossing the Pont d'Anglais suspension bridge over the Rivière de l'Est. When it was built in 1894 it was the longest bridge in the world.

The road descends for $6^1/_2$km (4 miles) to **Ste Rose** a coastal town whose defences were tested by the British in 1809 just prior to the taking of Reunion (*Bourbon*). The battle cost the life of Commodore Corbett of the British Fleet. A monument overlooking the sea just before reaching the town is erected in his memory.

The town lies in the foothills of the active volcano and several amazing sights attest to its activity. In 1977 the volcano disgorged its molten lava into the nearby village of Piton Ste Rose and destroyed many houses. There was no loss of life but the villagers watched entranced as the lava flow miraculously avoided the Notre-Dames des Laves Church, where it hardened to form a thick black girdle only inches from its front portals. From the village it is a short walk to the cascading waterfalls and cliffs of Anses des Cascades. A bar/restaurant provides vistas of the ocean and the comings and goings of locals in the fishing port of the same name.

STE ROSE TO ST JOSEPH (50KM, 31 MILES)

For the next 32km (20 miles) the RN2 negotiates the coast of the south-east under the shadow of the volcano to Ste Philippe. The road sweeps through the lush rainforest of Grand Brule. Every now and again, barren wastes indicate the lava paths left from previous eruptions. A few kilometres after leaving the village of **Bois Blanc** and before entering the forest, a statue of the Virgin Mary protecting her head with an open umbrella, suggests to the passing traveller that the area is subject to rain or shine. The statue *La Vierge au Parasol* (The Virgin With The Umbrella), was erected at the beginning of the twentieth century by a local landowner who believed it would protect the vanilla plantations from the fury of the volcano. It has since become a place of pilgrimage.

There are a number of walking trails through the Grand Brûlé Forest at Tremblet and Takamaka in the south-east. Here the Botanical Gardens of **St Philippe** may be reached by leaving the RN2 and taking the RF3 on the left towards the coast to Puits Arabe. The area is a coastal moonscape of hardened black lava created by nature following a tumultuous eruption in March 1986 when the lava solidified in the sea adding 30 hectares (74 acres) to the island's land mass. Here the visitor will find parking facilities, picnic sites and placards of historical and geological details of the eruption.

The area around St Philippe contains 70 hectares (174 acres) of tropical rainforest reserves which sweep inland to the volcano.

Walking trails from **Mare Longue** to the west of St Philippe zigzag to Tremblet on the east coast through thick plantations of pandanus and casuarina trees entwined with vanilla creepers, followed by mature mixed evergreen forests, locally termed, *bois de couleurs* (wood of many colours) and tall edible palms or *palmiste rouge*.

To the west of Mare Longue the RN2 passes a lava well called **Puits des Anglais**. The story goes that a veritable chest of treasure, watched over by the spirit of a dead slave, lies in its depths. Nearby is the Hotel Baril, the only hotel along this stretch of coast.

At **Le Cap Méchant** there are two cafés and restaurant overlooking the sea through lush forestland. Nearby is another well, called Puits des Français. The road continues to the little village of **Vicendo**. Take the road marked La Marine de Vicendo on the left to reach **Pointe Marcellin**. The road descends through cane fields and opens out to a forest of screwpines overlooking the ocean. At the end of the road there is a small statue of a white Virgin Mary with an inscription in French that translated says, 'Do whatever Jesus tells you'.

The next main town from St Philippe is **St Joseph** 18km (12 miles) with its old and modern architecture. Of particular interest is the church and the colonial style Mairie. The area is backed by gentle slopes of the vetyver plant, which provide essential ingredients for the manufacture of perfume. It is also used to make thatched roofs and baskets. The roots are taken to distilleries at sugar cane factories where from May to December the air is thick with scent.

The Rivière des Remparts flows through the town with its source 20km (12 miles) inland from Nez de Boeuf on the outer rim of the volcano. Lovely walks can be made along the banks of the river and swimmers may enjoy a refreshing dip in the natural ponds. From St Joseph walks can be made to Manapany and Langevin.

After St Joseph follow the RN2 around the coast for 7km (4 miles) where there is a turn off (D31) for **Petite Ile**. Here there is a distillation centre and at **Grande Anse** back on the RN2 there are beach and camping facilities.

ST JOSEPH TO ST LEU (50KM, 31 MILES)

After leaving St Joseph the area of the volcano is left behind. Ahead lie more gentle slopes and a wide coastal plain. The RN2 hugs the coast for 9km (6 miles) beaches and lagoon of **St Pierre**, an important town lying at the mouth of the Rivière d'Abord. The river follows the route of the RN3 inland to Plaine des Palmiste.

The Hôtel de Ville, is a beautiful example of colonial architecture. To the west of town at **La Ravine Blanche** is the Tamil temple of

Narassiga-Peroumal. It is possible to make a small detour to the fishing port of Terre Sainte which is partially hidden by banyan trees.

On leaving St Pierre the road changes its identity to become the RN1 and all signposts are for St Denis. Although there are alternative roads which go inland and pass through various villages the RN1 remains close to the sea offering many viewpoints.

The dull and unattractive town of **St Louis** is 11km (7 miles) from St Pierre, bordered to the east by the wide estuary of Rivière St Etienne. The town itself has little of interest save for the island's oldest church dating back to 1733. The lack of hotels and restaurants make it more of a starting point than a tourist attraction for excursions to the Cilaos cirque and the surrounding area. A detour may be made by taking the CD20 from the centre of town to **Les Makes**, a tiny village situated at 1,000m (3,280ft) with magnificent views of the Cilaos cirque. Return on the CD23 to St Louis via Le Gol-les-Hauts and the village of La Rivière where skilled craftsmen make fine reproductions of French colonial furniture.

One of the island's four sugar factories is located on the right of the RN1 just outside St Louis. The Usine de Gol is the only sugar factory on the western coast.

From St Louis it is 10km (6 miles) to the coastal resort town of **L'Étang-Salé les Bains** and Le Gouffre, where the sea is compressed into rapids of white water by narrow rock crevices. Further along the coast there are lovely black beaches and watersports facilities. In the town there are the remains of the island's only railway. Built in the late nineteenth century it ran a coastal route for 35km (22 miles) from St Pierre to St Benoit. However the cost of running the railway was so high that the line was disbanded in the early 1960s.

Take the CD17 from the town to reach the magnificent forest of **Etang-Salé.** Here there is a campsite, picnic areas, a nine-hole golf course, facilities for pigeon shooting and a bird park. The bird park lying in 2 hectares (5 acres) of land contains some beautiful local and exotic species. At the exit of the bird park signs indicate the area of Gol which is renowned for its hand-made wicker chairs manufactured from local wood and wild rushes.

A detour may be made inland from Bois-Blanc which connects with the CD11 to the dairy farming area of **Les Avirons** where there are panoramic views of the ocean. From Les Avirons the CD11 winds north and just outside St Leu joins again with the RN1. However if this route north is taken then the water spouts, as described in the following paragraph will have been missed.

The RN1 slices through a jagged expanse of black lava rock which meets the powerful Indian Ocean breakers. Here parking areas provide spectacular views of water spouts or *souffleurs*.

Continuing north on the RN1 the land and coastal scenery alters considerably after the Pointe au Sel. The plain widens to some 10km (6 miles) in places and much of the coast is protected by large stretches of coral reef and many golden beaches.

St Leu is a former coffee growing area where slaves revolted in 1811. In 1859 the inhabitants were saved from an outbreak of cholera that accompanied a ship bringing Mozambique labourers to the island. The epidemic nearly wiped out the population of St Denis and St Louis, miraculously avoiding St Leu. A pilgrimage to the Church and Chapel of Notre-Dame de la Salette takes place on 19 September each year.

In the town there are lovely views of the coast from the Church of Colimacons, built in 1875 by a local family. The Hôtel de Ville is amongst the few remaining buildings constructed entirely of stone.

Just out of the town on the coast side turtles from the Indian islands of Tromelin and Europa are commercially bred at La Ferme Tortue Corail.

LA SALINE LES BAINS TO ST PAUL (26KM, 16 MILES)

Twelve kilometres (7 miles) after St Leu is the resort of **La Saline les Bains**. The RN1 follows the contours of several wide headlands which allow the land to be extended forming the very widest coastal plain of the island. Just before La Saline les Bains a well formed reef begins and shadows the coast, almost unbroken, to Cape La Houssaye. Blessed with these attributes and a near perfect year round climate it is not surprising that this area is the most sought after by sun seekers.

From La Saline les Bains it is $4^1/_2$km (3 miles) to the seaside resort of **St Gilles les Bains** and Boucan Canot. The former, with its fishing harbour and Yacht Club, has been dubbed the St Tropez of the Indian Ocean and panders to every whim of the sun and pleasure seeker. Accommodation ranges from the modern four-star Mascareigne Grand Hotel to the rather less pretentious but comfortable Village de Vacances self-catering bungalows and a campsite. The larger hotels can organise big game fishing expeditions in crewed boats or individuals may enquire direct at the Centre de Peche in the port of St Gilles. In addition the resort boasts excellent water sports facilities from windsurfing, water skiing and skin diving to just lazing on the beach or gazing at underwater life from a glass bottom boat while horse-riders can enjoy the facilities offered inland at the Centre Equestre de l'Hermitage.

Reunion is a paradise for walking enthusiasts

Big game fishing boats at St Pierre

Boucan Canot, easily accessible from the capital of St Denis and made all the more attractive by its white beaches and lagoon, can be extremely crowded at the weekends.

After St Gilles les Bains the road follows the contour of the Cape Homard and La Houssaye to the large town of **St Paul** where the black volcanic sands indicate an absence of coral reef. It is a popular holiday resort being within easy distance of the yellow beaches of Boucan Canot and St Gilles and gives easy access to some wonderful inland scenery and sites of touristical interest.

St Paul was the former capital of Reunion and was of great importance to the French East India Company who established their headquarters in the grand colonial building which is now the Mairie. The town is particularly lively on Saturday mornings when locals hold an open-air market on the seafront.

From St Paul the road becomes a motorway for the 22km (13 miles) journey to St Denis and passes the **Grotte des Premiers Francais** where the mutineers from Madagascar spent their first night in 1646. Further on is the Marine Cemetery one of the oldest on the island. It is the burial place of the most famous of pirates, Olivier Le Vasseur, better known as La Buse, who attacked any vessel in the Indian Ocean and infuriated the East India Companies by carrying off the booty to some secret destination. He was sent to the gallows in 1730 and never revealed where his treasure was buried. His tomb has a cross with a skull and crossbones.

After St Paul the motorway crosses the very wide estuary of Rivière des Galets, bypasses the coastal town of Le Port and emerges back on to the coast at La Possession. From La Possession the motorway clings to the cliffs and is made in the mould of true riviera corniche dimensions as it approaches St Denis. In fact it is known as La Corniche and this 14km (9 mile) race track is without doubt the busiest stretch of road in the Indian Ocean.

ST DENIS

In 1738 the French East Indies Company transferred its headquarters from St Paul to St Denis. In spite of St Denis becoming the principal town it took several centuries to develop as a capital. Isolated by high mountains and lack of harbour facilities, poor roads and inadequate street lighting, it lay neglected for years. In the late 1950s it was described as being ill equipped to receive any tourists and those that were sheltered at one of the capital's two hotels.

Since the island was administered as a French overseas department, St Denis has changed from a down-at-heel backwater into a

168 • Visitor's Guide: Mauritius, Rodrigues & Reunion

sophisticated capital and offers the visitor all the facilities of any major town in Metropolitan France. If Reunion is the little France of the Indian Ocean then St Denis deserves to be called the little Paris. Its excellent roads link the capital with the beaches of the south-west and an efficient public transport system enables easy access to the interior. Hotels, pensions and guest houses, shops and restaurants make it an excellent base for a few days stay.

St Denis is the main administrative and commercial centre. The town straddles the mouth of the Rivière St Denis and sweeps upwards into the flanks of La Montagne where modern apartment blocks and luxurious houses have replaced the shanty town of the post war era. The heart of the town lies east of the Rivière St Denis.

There are few parking restrictions in the town. It may be convenient to park at Le Barachois on the sea front and continue by foot. At **Le Barachois** there is promenade and gardens with two old cannon facing out to sea. Nearby is Le Meridien Hotel and casino. Looking inland from the sea to the right of the hotel is a statue of Roland Garros, the famous aviator, who was born in St Denis. Continue past the statue to the Hotel de la Prefecture, a grand colonial building dating back to 1733 and the former headquarters of the French East Indies Company.

Just in front of the Hotel de la Prefecture is a statue of Mahe de Labourdonnais, who as in Port Louis, stares solemnly out to the Indian Ocean. In Avenue de la Victoire are several notable buildings. On the right at the junction with Rue de Labourdonnais is the cathedral, dating back to 1832, which was built on the site of a former church. The fountain was added later in 1854.

Almost opposite the cathedral is the university which was built in 1759 as a college for the Lazarist Order. It was later used as a barracks, marine office and maternity hospital. On the same side of the road is the beautifully preserved Hôtel de Ville. Built in 1860 and used until 1977, the interior courtyard has a striking bronze fountain.

The Victory Monument, in Avenue de la Victoire commemorates the French soldiers who died in both World Wars. Beyond it, the avenue continues as Rue de Paris where the **Museum of Leon Dieux** is situated on the right. The museum was the former Episcopal Palace constructed in 1846. It contains paintings of great artists including Cezanne, Gaugin, Picasso, Renoir, Rodin and Manet.

At the end of Rue de Paris is the **Jardin de l'Etat** (State Gardens). The gardens were created by the French botanist Nicolas Bréon in 1817 and contain hundreds of exotic plants and trees in an area of over 5 hectares (12 acres). Every 7 years St Denis hosts the Indian Ocean Flower Show at the gardens. The event was last held in 1987 and was attended by hundreds of visitors from all over the world.

Go through to the end of the gardens to reach the **Natural History Museum**. The building dates back to 1855 and used to be the colonial headquarters. The museum contains superb displays of rare marine fauna, including the Coelanthe, an enormous fish weighing 300kg, which was caught in the Comores Islands in 1938. On the first floor are displays of extinct birds including the dodo of Mauritius.

There are several interesting markets held daily in St Denis, notably the Covered Market on the corner of Rue Marechal Street and Rue Lucien Gasparin and the outdoor market at **Chaudron** to the east of the town. Both are lively affairs with gaily coloured stalls of fruit and vegetables, handicrafts, basketwork and embroidery. The main shopping areas are in Rue Marechal Leclerc and Rue Labourdonnais.

St Denis is a good centre to sample the various restaurants which specialise in French, Indian and Chinese cuisine while small bars, cafeterias and market stalls provide delicacies such as *bonbon piment* (fritters fried with crushed peas and chilli) and samousas (triangular shaped pastries stuffed with vegetables, meat or fish). Throughout the island the visitor will come across Reunionese cuisine either in towns and villages or at hotels. The food is typically spicy and consists of delicious *carri* (curry) made from meat, fish or chicken and is traditionally served with white rice, pulses, *brèdes* (similar to greens) and *achard* (a fierce vegetable chutney flavoured with chillis).

Additional Information

Bras-Panon
Coop Vanille
Open: 8am-11.30am and 2-4.30pm.

Etang-Salé
Jardin d' Oiseaux (Bird Park)
Open: every day, except public holidays, 8am-6pm.

Hell-Bourg
Parc Pisciole (Trout Farm)
Open: every day, except public holidays, 8am-6pm.
Admission free.
☎ 23 50 16

St Denis
Jardin de l' Etat
Open: every day, 6am-6pm.
Admission free.

Natural History Museum
Open: Monday to Friday, 10am-4pm. Admission free.
☎ 20 02 19

Museum of Leon-Dieux
Open: Monday to Friday, except Tuesday and public holidays, 10am-12noon and 3pm-6pm.

St Gilles les Bains
Centre de Peche
Open: every day from 10am-6pm.
☎ 24 62 84 or 24 02 02

St Leu
La Ferme Tortue Corail (Turtle Farm)
Open: every day, except public
holidays, 8am-12noon and 2pm-
5pm. Admission charge.

Useful Addresses

Tourist Information Centres
Main tourist office on Reunion
Comité du Tourisme de la Réunion
Residence Vetyver
23 Rue Tourette (first floor)
97400
St Denis
☎ 41 84 41 or 21 00 41

Local Tourist Offices on Reunion
(Offices de Tourisme Syndicats
d'Initiative):

St Denis
Maison de la Montagne
10 Place de la Sarda Garriga
☎ 21 75 84

St Pierre
27 Rue Archambaud
☎ 25 02 36

St Benoit
Rue Montfleury
☎ 50 10 65

Bras-Panon
Co-operative de Vanille
☎ 51 10 62

St Gilles les Baines
Galleries Amandine
☎ 24 57 47

St Paul
Avenue de la Gare
☎ 45 45 23

La Plaine des Palmistes
Rue de la Republic
☎ 51 32 57

Cilaos
4 Rue des Ecoles
☎ 31 78 03

Maison de la Montagne
Rue du Père Boiteau
☎ 31 71 55

Salazie
Relais des Cimes
Hellbourg
☎ 47 50 09

St André
La Mairie
Avenue Île de France
☎ 46 91 63

Helicopter Tours

Air Réunion
☎ 20 27 27

Heli-Lagon
☎ 55 55 55

Sud Aero-Service
☎ 25 78 00

Mauritius Fact File

Accommodation

Accommodation ranges from luxury hotels to simple guest houses.
Hotels are presently not star rated although a rating system should be
introduced by 1992. Hotels owned by the Beachcomber, Sun International and Pullman groups are in the luxury range and include free
sporting facilities with the exception of scuba diving and deep sea
fishing. They are located on the best beaches with lush gardens and
provide first class cuisine and entertainment. Smaller hotels on the
west and north-west coasts are geared to family holidays with
generally good accommodation and facilities.

Small guesthouses provide simple accommodation. Many are in
the Mahebourg area and make an ideal base for exploring the
remote southern coast. Breakfast is not always included in the
price and any extra meals may have to be ordered in advance.

Beachside bungalows are available for long or short term rental
and often include maid service. The Mauritian Government
Tourist Office publish a booklet of budget accommodation with
tarrifs and details of tour companies offering holidays in Mauritius. A useful address in the UK is V. Moonoosamy, 2 Far
Headingley Court, Headingly Street, off Moor Road, Headingley,
Leeds IS6 4BK, West Yorkshire ☎ (0532) 754721 who can arrange
private self catering accommodation. In Mauritius, there are rental
agencies in the Grand Baie area but many locals place a sign
outside their bungalow indicating that it is available for rent or
advertise in the newspaper.

Banks

Banks are normally open from 10am to 2pm Monday to Friday and 9.30
to 11.30am on Saturdays. Most accept travellers cheques and Eurocheques.

The Mauritius Commercial Bank at Grand Baie is open from 8am to
6pm Monday to Saturday and from 9am to 2pm on Sundays and
public holidays. Their branch at Curepipe is open 9.30am to 5pm
Monday to Saturday. In addition cash can be obtained at any of their
'Mr Best' dispensers by inserting either Access or Mastercard credit
cards and keying in the personal identification number.

Barclays Bank at Grand Baie, Curepipe and Port Louis is open from
9.30am to 2.30pm Monday to Saturday.

Cash advances of up to 2,600 rupees per day can be made on production of passport and Mastercard (Access) or Barclaycard (Visa) at all branches of the Mauritius Commercial Bank and Barclays Bank respectively. All banks have their head offices at Port Louis and branches in the plateau towns and some villages. Most have a separate counter for foreign exchange.

Hotels accept major credit cards such as American Express, Diners, Barclaycard and Access and offer exchange facilities although banks give a better deal.

A passport should be produced for all transactions and visitors are advised to retain receipts to enable them to change rupees back to foreign currency.

Camera Equipment

Sparkling white sand, turquoise seas and brilliant blue skies contrasting with the colourful dress of dark skinned Mauritians provide stunning pictures. But these are the very ingredients which may play havoc with auto exposure programmes on single lens reflex and compact cameras. The dense dark green foliage against sunlit sky can induce similar problems so careful metering and even bracketing help provide the perfect shots one expects from such a photogenic location.

Fuji, Kodak and Agfa processing laboratories are found in Port Louis and the plateau towns. Results are generally good but the range of size of prints is limited. All types of film, well known makes of camera and limited accessories are available in camera shops in Port Louis. Be prepared for high prices. Try to take the equipment you might need with you.

A lens hood and/or polarising filter are very useful accessories to reduce flare from brilliant sunshine and reflection from bright colours. Great effects can be produced by shooting straight into the sun and a graduated grey filter allows you to do this without over exposure. With high temperatures and humidity all equipment should, if possible, be adequately protected with silicon crystals and kept in an insulated bag. A camera left in the mid-day sun for only a few minutes can result in a fogged film. If professional film is used it must be kept refrigerated both before and after use but to be safe the same precaution may be applied to all emulsions.

Mauritians normally respond well to being photographed. Ask for permission if in doubt. A very useful organisation in Port Louis (PO Box 1051) is the Association de l'Art Photographique de l'Ile Maurice (AAPIM) who organise outings, slide shows and meetings of interest to visiting professional and amateur photographers. Contact: Steeve Dubois, President on ☎ 208 3840 after 5pm for details.

Chemists

Pharmacies are found in all towns and most villages. They stock most medical supplies and medicines although familiar brand names may not be readily available. There is no restriction on prescribed medicines for personal use.

Consult the Sunday newspaper for emergency chemists under the heading 'Pharmacies de Garde'. A list of duty chemists is normally displayed on the notice boards of Town Halls.

Climate

Mauritius enjoys a tropical maritime climate which can be divided into two seasons: summer and winter.

The hot summer months from November to April produce prolonged sunshine with temperatures of up to 35 °C (95 °F) on the coasts which may be broken by short heavy bursts of rainfall. Humidity is to be high even at night. From May to October autumnal conditions are accompanied by temperatures of up to 25 °C (77 °F) with cooler nights and less humidity. The south-east trade winds blow all year keeping the south and east coasts cool during the summer months but they can be uncomfortably windy during the rest of the year.

Cyclones, known as hurricanes or typhoons in the northern hemisphere, occur occasionally between December and April. These tropical depressions are born hundreds of miles to the north-east of Mauritius and take days to meander westwards. Various weather stations track their route and warnings that a cyclone may develop are broadcast days in advance. Most pass by harmlessly bringing only heavy rain and serving to clear the air after a spell of very hot humid weather. Tourists in their sturdily built hotels are rarely troubled by the conditions and are advised regarding the suitability of drinking tap water following a cyclone. Bottled water is available in hotels and supermarkets.

The differences in altitude, topography and wind direction produce varied micro-climates with the result that the towns of the central plateau are often cloud capped and damp while the coast is clear and sunny. These higher regions may provide temperatures of up to 5 °C (9 °F) cooler than coastal areas.

Mauritius has a good year round climate for visitors but for those who like to walk, tour, and explore the best time to visit is October and November. These are the driest months and provide less humidity than high summer. They are also outside the cyclone season. There is little difference in terms of sunshine and air and sea temperatures are not excessive.

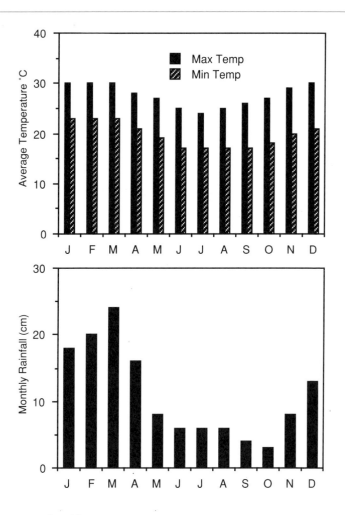

Communications

Post

The postal service is efficient and all staff speak English.
Post Offices operate in most towns and villages.
Post Office Headquarters: Quay Street, Port Louis ☎ 208 2851
Opening hours are Monday to Friday 8-11am, 12noon-4pm. Saturday 8am-12noon.

Telephones

International Direct Dialing services are available. The code for Mauritius is 230.

Overseas telephone calls can be made and telexes sent from the Overseas Telephone Service (OTS) located at the side entrance of Rogers House in Port Louis. The clerk on duty obtains the number required and the call is taken in a private cubicle. Payment is made at the conclusion of the call and a receipt is provided. The office is open from 8.30am to 5pm Monday to Friday and 8.30am to 2pm on Saturday. A 24-hour service is provided at the OTS office at Cassis, about 1km ($^1/_2$ mile) to the west of Port Louis.

To make an overseas call from a private telephone, dial 00, followed by the country code, area code, and the telephone number required. Telephone facilities exist at all hotels although expect to pay heavy commission charges. Some shopkeepers may allow use of their telephone for local calls. Public call boxes can be found at main post offices and police stations but ensure you have enough.

All telephone numbers in Mauritius should have seven figures by 1992. In cases of difficulty dial 90 for local Directory Enquiries.

To book a call dial 10 091, for International Enquiries dial 10 092, for International Directory Information dial 10 090. All telephone operators speak English.

Main international direct dialling codes are: Australia 010 (61), UK 010 (44) Canada and USA 010(1).

Currency and Credit Cards

There is no limit on the amount of foreign currency brought into the country in the form of travellers cheques, bankers drafts or letters of credit. Travellers may import Mauritian notes to the maximum of 700Rs and take out 350Rs. Major credit cards are accepted at banks and most shops and restaurants.

The monetary unit is the Mauritian Rupee (Rs) which is divided into 100 cents (cs). There are 1-rupee pieces, 5, 10, 20, 25, 50 cent-pieces. Notes come in the following denominations: Rs 5, 10, 50, 100, 200, 500, and Rs 1,000. Foreign currency notes, drafts, travellers cheque and other banking instruments may be imported into Mauritius without restriction.

Customs Regulations

Passengers of 16 years of age and over may import duty free: 250 grammes of tobacco (including cigars and cigarettes), 2 litres of spirits, 2 litres of wine, ale or beer, one quarter litre of toilet water and a quantity of perfume not exceeding 10cl.

A plant import permit must be obtained from the Ministry of Agriculture, Fisheries and Natural Resources, prior to the introduction of plants and plant material including cuttings, flowers, bulbs, fresh fruits, vegetables and seeds. All plant material must be declared to Customs immediately on arrival and is subject to examination.

Facilities for examination and certification of plant materials are available at Réduit (☎ 454 1091), Mer Rouge Port Louis (☎ 242 4127) and Sir Seewoosagur Ramgoolam International Airport offices of the Plant Pathology Division of the Ministry of Agriculture, Fisheries and Natural Resources (☎ 6373 194).

All animals including animal material need an import permit from the Ministry of Agriculture, Fisheries and Natural Resources, and a sanitary certificate of country of origin. All animals must be declared to the Customs immediately on arrival and landing is only allowed if certificates issued by the Veterinary Authorities of the exporting country is in conformity with the Import Permit. Dogs and cats undergo a 6 months' quarantine. Birds and other animal species up to 2 months.

Additional information may be obtained from the Division of Veterinary Services of the Ministry of Agriculture, Fisheries and Natural Resources Réduit (☎ 454 1016). For animal and plant inspection and delivery permits contact
Agricultural Services, Head Office, Réduit ☎ 454 1016.

Firearms and ammunitions must be declared on arrival. Drug trafficking still carries the death penalty. A compulsory airport tax of 100Rs is levied on all departing passengers, except for those travelling to Rodrigues.

Electricity

Electricity is 220V. Plugs, adaptors and batteries are available for electrical equipment. Power cuts are inevitable in the cyclone season and as roads are poorly lit at night it is advisable to take a torch.

Embassies and High Commissions

Australia
Mauritius High Commission
43 Hampton Circuit
Yarralumla ACT 2600
Canberra
☎ (06) 281 1203 and (06) 282 4436

UK
Mauritius High Commission
32/33 Elvaston Place
London SW7
☎ (071) 581 0294
  and (071) 581 0295

USA
Mauritius Embassy
Suite 134
Van Ness Centre
4301 Connecticut Avenue, NW
Washington DC 20008
☎ 202 244 1491 92

High Commissions in Mauritus
are as follows:
Australia
High Commission
Rogers House
President John Kennedy Street
Port Louis
☎ 208 1700

Canada
High Commission
c/o Blance Birger Company Ltd
Jules Koenig Street
Port Louis
☎ 208 0821

UK
High Commission
King Georges V Avenue
Floreal
☎ 686 5795

USA
4th floor, Rogers House
President John Kennedy Street
Port Louis
☎ 208 2347

Emergencies

Police, Fire and Ambulance dial 999 and ask for the service required.
Callers will be connected to the nearest control. Give precise details of
the incident and the address where help is needed. The following
numbers are useful in non urgent cases:

Police
Port Louis District Headquarters
☎ 208 1212

*Pamplemousses and Rivière du
Rempart District Headquarters*
(Grand Baie, Trou aux Biches,
Tombeau Bay, Poudre d'Or,
Triolet and Goodlands)
☎ 264 1536

*Grand Port and Savanne District
Headquarters*
(Mahebourg, Souillac, Plaisance,
Baie du Cap, Nouvelle France)
☎ 627 4669

*Plaines Wilhelms and Black River
District Headquarters*
(Curepipe, Rose Hill, Beau
Bassin, Quatre Bornes, Bambous,
Black River)
☎ 454 2022

*Upper Plaines Wilhelms District
Headquarters*
(Floreal, Phoenix and Vacoas)
☎ 675 3031

Moku and Flaq District Headquarters
(Quartier Militaire, Trou d'Eau
Douce, Le Réduit, St Pierre, Flaq)
☎ 433 3301

Facilities For The Disabled

Disabled people will find facilities in the large hotels generally very good. Ramps and concrete walkways blend into manicured tropical gardens of beachside complexes and there is good wheelchair access to rooms, corridors and reception areas. For specific information visitors are advised to consult their travel agent.

Festivals and Local Events

Many public holidays are movable feasts so enquire at the tourist office who publish a monthly 'What's On' or at the local town hall. Cultural centres have their own programme of events. *Le Grand Baie News*, a monthly listings magazine, published in French and English, is available free from shops and hotels in the Grand Baie area.

Illness and Injury

Emergency hospital treatment is free and there are a number of private clinics. The larger hotels have a resident doctor. Local doctors will attend cases of sudden illness. Avoid contact with stray dogs and if bitten seek medical advice as soon as possible.

Avoid wading in muddy waters without wearing protective shoes. This is the habitat of the laff or stone fish which if trodden upon emits a poisonous venom from its spines. Local fishermen resort to a poultice remedy but immediate removal to hospital is necessary as the wound can be fatal if untreated.

Private Clinics
Quatre Bornes
Stevenson Street
☎ 425 0423

Curepipe
De Lorette
Higginson Street
☎ 675 2911

Dr Darne
Curepipe Road
☎ 686 1477

Rose Hill
Bon Pasteur
Thomy Pitot Street
☎ 464 2640

Réduit
Mauricienne
☎ 454 3061

Public Hospitals
Port Louis
Dr A. G. Jeetoo Hospital
Volcy Pougnet Street
☎ 212 3201

Pamplemousses
SSR National Hospital
☎ 264 1661

Mahebourg
Mahebourg Hospital
Princess Margaret Hospital
☎ 631 9556

Rose Belle
Jawaharlal Nehru Hospital
☎ 627 4960

Moka
Eye Hospital
☎ 433 4015

Quatre Bornes
Princess Margaret Hospital
☎ 454 3031

Vacoas
☎ 686 2061

Vaccination Centres
Port Louis
Victoria Square
☎ 212 3221

Air Mauritius
5 John Kennedy Street
Rogers House
☎ 208 7700

Language

The lingua franca is Creole which is a derivative of French. The official language is English although French is widely spoken. In addition there are various Indian and Chinese languages. It is not uncommon to hear a mixture of both French and English words or phrases spoken in one sentence. In this book, place names in Mauritius and Rodrigues have been shown in their most commonly used form, which may be in either French or English. When asking for directions, particularly in the case of rivers, bays and mountains, the use of either language will be understood, eg, Pointe aux Cannoniers or Cannonier's Point, Tombeau Bay or Baie du Tombeau, Rivière Noire or Black River, English Bay or Anse aux Anglais.

English language newspapers are available to customers awaiting transactions in some major banks in Port Louis. There are plenty of local newspapers, the most popular being the morning *L'Express* and the evening *Le Mauricien*. Both are published in French with some news items and advertisements in English.

The Mauritius Broadcasting Corporation (MaBC) transmits television news in English at 5.40pm and radio news at 8am, 3pm and 9pm every day. BBC World Service can be received on various frequencies, mainly in the morning and late evening.

The following newspapers are available to UK and overseas subscribers and give good coverage of Mauritian affairs at home and abroad.

Mauritian International
2A Vant Road
London SW17
☎ (081) 767 2439

Mauritius News
PO Box 26
London SE17 1GG
☎ (071) 703 1071

Legal Advice

If you are arrested and need legal representation contact the relevant diplomatic mission listed on pages 176 and 177. However it should be stressed that they cannot normally personally advise on legal matters but may assist with regard to finding an interpreter or contacting friends or relatives.

Maps

Pocket size maps are available in bookshops in Port Louis and most hotel boutiques although these will only highlight tourist spots. A more detailed and accurate map published by the Government of Mauritius, is available from Edward Stanford Limited, 12/14 Long Acre, Covent Garden, London WC2E 9LP ☎ (071) 8361321. In Mauritius copies are available to the public from the third floor of the Ministry of Housing, Lands and the Environment, Edith Cavell Street, Port Louis. The *French Institut Geographique National No 5/15* is not as accurate as the official Government map but may be easier to obtain in Europe.

Measurements

The metric system is used in Mauritius. Conversions are:
1 kilogram (1,000 grams) = 2.2lb
1 litre = $1^3/_4$ pints
4.5 litres = 1 gallon
8km = 5 miles
Weights are often measured in pounds.

National Holidays

New Year's Day — 1 and 2 January
Chinese Spring Festival — February/March (variable)
Cavadee — mid-January (variable)
Maha Shivaratree — February/March (variable)
Independence Day — 12 March
Ougadi — March/April (variable)
Labour Day — 1 May
Id El Fitr — May/June (variable)
Ganesh Chaturthi — September
Divali — October/November (variable)
All Saints Day — 1 November
Christmas Day — 25 December

Passports and Visas

Nationals of the EEC, USA, Japan, South Africa, Zimbabwe and all Commonwealth countries do not require visas. Other nationals or those in doubt should enquire at the Embassy or High Commission. Entry is normally granted for up to 30 days and visitors must produce a return or onward ticket of their next destination. Extensions of stay may be applied for at the Police Immigration Department, Line Barracks, Port Louis with two passport size photographs and evidence that visitors do not intend to be a burden on the state. There is no charge for an extension visa. The office is open Monday to Friday 10am-12noon and 2 to 2.30pm and Saturdays 10am to 11.30am.

Personal Insurance and Medical Cover

Vaccination certificates are required if coming from an infected area. Malaria has been eradicated but occasionally there are isolated outbreaks. Check with a doctor or travel agent prior to departure for the latest requirements. Regulations are strict, particularly for those arriving from Africa.

Dental and medical facilities are very good and most practitioners speak English. The cost of treatment is substantially less than European countries although it is advisable to take out private medical insurance to cover repatriation expenses.

The services of opticians and contact lens practitioners are widely available and of a good standard. Spectacles are good value and prescriptions can be made up in a few days.

Public Toilets

Public toilets are generally unlocked and are situated at bus stations, town markets and public beaches. Signs are in English and marked 'Toilet' or 'WC'. Most restaurant and bar owners and staff in office buildings and shops allow visitors use of the toilet which is normally kept under lock and key. Always carry toilet paper with you. If attended, a few rupees is apreciated.

Religion

The family unit in Mauritius is such that children are welcome at all social and religious gatherings and no objection would be raised to foreign children taking part. A decent standard of dress is required when visiting places of worship and the removal of shoes is appreciated when entering a mosque or temple.

Mosques, temples and churches standing almost side by side reflect the religious tolerance of the country's multi cultural society. The main religions are Christianity, Hinduism and Islam and colourful religious festivals are observed and enjoyed by all year round.

Mass can be observed at St Louis Cathedral in Port Louis as well as in towns and small villages throughout the island. The Church of England has the following churches: St James at Port Louis, Holy Trinity at Rose Hill and St Andrews at Quatre Bornes. Presbyterian services are held in Rose Hill and Curepipe and at St Columba's Church at Vacoas with English service on Sundays at 9.30am. There is a Church of the Seventh Day Adventists in Rose Hill.

Mauritians, being such a mixed people, are proud of their racial and religious harmony. Most political subjects can be freely discussed and are given a good airing in a lively press.

Shopping

Supermarkets stock a wide range of local and imported goods. The small local shop known as *la boutik* is a feature of every Mauritian town and village where essential foodstuffs, including alcohol and some toiletries can be bought.

Shops in the plateau towns are open from 9am-6pm, Monday to Wednesday, and Saturday, with early closing at 1pm on Thursdays and late night shopping till 9.30pm on Fridays. Port Louis shops are open from 9am-5pm Monday to Friday with early closing at 12noon on Saturdays. There are daily food markets in Port Louis and most towns. Quatre Bornes holds its twice weekly *foire* or market on Wednesdays and Saturdays.

Plenty of bargains are found in knitwear, shirts and dresses at substantially lower prices than at home. Most hotels can provide information on where to buy handmade replicas of old sailing ships and the purchase of duty free diamonds.

Bartering, except with market traders and beach hawkers, is unlikely to succeed.

Sports and Pastimes

Beach Guide

All beaches are open to the public although access via hotel entrances may be restricted. Public beaches can get crowded at weekends and holidays. In the north public beaches include Baie du Tombeau, Balaclava, Pereybere, Troux aux Biches, Mon Choisy, Grand Baie, Bain Boeufs and Cap Malheureux. In the south are Riambel, Baie du

Cap, La Prairie and Blue Bay. The east coast has Belle Mare, Poste Lafayette and Isle aux Cerfs and the west has Pointe aux Sables, Albion, Flic en Flac, Tamarin, Le Morne and Rivière Noire.

Boating and Sailing, Water and Land Sports

Grand Baie
Yacht Club
☎ 263 8945
Only open to visiting yachtsmen.

Centre Nautique de Grand Baie
☎ 263 8017
Open: 8am-5pm.
Hire of windsurf, water-ski equipment.

Yacht Charters Limited
☎ 263 8395/6
Open: 8am-5pm.
Excursions in tall ship, *Isla Mauritia*, around island.

Tara Charters & Tours
Royal Road
☎ 263 7948
Open: 8am-5pm.
Catamaran yacht cruises.

Paradise Diving
☎ 263 7220
Open: 8.30am-5pm.
Sailing, scuba diving, water ski, paragliding, yacht charter.

Phoenix
Mauritius Underwater Group
Railway Road
☎ 696 5368
Open: Monday to Saturday 8am-8pm. Sundays and public

holidays 8am-12noon. Tuesday club night 8am-11.30pm. Share premises with Mauritius Marine Conservation Society. Clubhouse and bar. Affiliated to British Sub-Aqua club. Temporary membership for visitors.

Dive centres are located at hotels which also provide water and land sport facilities. For a full list contact the Mauritius Government Tourist Office. The use of a harpoon is strictly forbidden.

Trou aux Biches
Organisation de Pêche du Nord
Le Corsaire Club
Open: 8.30am-5pm.
☎ 261 6267/6264
Big game fishing specialists

Black River
Rivière Noire Hotel
☎ 683 6547
Open: 8.30am-5pm (or through hotel reception).
Big game fishing specialists.

Centre de Peche de Rivière Noire
Hotel Club
☎ 683 6503
Big game fishing specialist.

Excursions
The following organise excursions throughout the island and have offices at major hotels.

Port Louis
White Sand Tours
La Chaussée
☎ 2 3712

Mauritius Travel and Tourist
   Bureau
Rue Royal
☎ 208 2041

Rose Hill
Mauritours
Rue Venkatasananda
☎ 454 3078
(walking tours)

Tourist Information Centres

Australia
Mauritius Tourist Information
   Bureau
313 Abernethy Road
Belmont 6104
Perth
☎ (09) 479 1708

UK
Mauritius Government Tourist
   Office
32/33 Elvaston Place
London SW7
☎ (071) 584 3666

USA
Mauritius Government Tourist
   Office
c/o Pask Associates Inc
15 Penn Plaza
415 Seventh Avenue
New York
NY 10001
☎ (212) 239 8350

Travel

By Air
Mauritius is well served by air. Several airlines connect with Sir
Seewoosagur Ramgoolam International Airport (Plaisance). Air
Mauritius flies from London, Paris, Amsterdam, Rome, Munich,
Frankfurt, Zurich, Geneva, Nairobi, Johannesburg, Durban, Harare,
Singapore, Hong Kong, Kuala Lumpur, Moroni, Madagascar,
Reunion and Rodrigues. British Airways and Air Mauritius fly direct
from London (Heathrow) taking 12 hours. Air France, with connect-
ing flights at Paris, also make the journey normally with stopovers.
Mauritius is also served by Lufthansa, South African Airways, Air
India, Air Madagascar, Singapore Airlines, Air Tanzania, Air Zimba-
bwe and Zambia Airways.

Flight information may be obtained from the following Air Mauritius
offices.

UK
Air Mauritius
49 Conduit Street
London W1R 9FB
☎ (071) 434 4375

Canada
Air Mauritius
750 Airways Centre Business Park
5925 Airport Road
Mississauga
Ontario L4V 1WI
☎ (416) 405 0188

Australia
Air Mauritius
Suite 1204, MLC Centre
Level 12/19 to 29 Martin Place
GPO Box 5064
Sydney NSW2001
☎ (02) 22 17 300

Profesional Travel Services Pty Ltd
1205 Hay Street
West Perth
WA 6005
☎ (09) 481 0888

USA
Air Mauritius
617 Olive Street
Suite 807
Los Angeles
California 90014
☎ (213) 893 7375

Air Mauritius
560 Sylvia Avenue
Englewood Cliffs
New Jersey 07632
☎ (201) 871 8382
 (USA only: 800 5371182)

There is a branch of the Mauritius Government Tourist Office at the airport. The main office is located at Emmanuel Anquetil Building, Sir Seewoosagur Ramgoolam Street, Port Louis ☎ 201 1703. The airport is located in the south of the island. It is modern, bright and spacious with duty free shopping for arriving visitors, banks and car hire facilities. Members of the public are restricted to the waiting area outside the airport building. Buses only link with Curepipe where changes will have to be made if travelling to other parts of the island. Taxis are available but as they are meterless, agree a price before starting any journey.

The fastest way of seeing the island is on an organised tour and in some cases, the only way, as prior permission has to be obtained from the landowners. The prices often include meals as appropriate and the services of a knowledgeable guide and comfortable transport. Air Mauritius jet ranger helicopters seating four persons offer sightseeing tours of up to one hour's duration from major hotels.

By Bus
For those who would rather travel independently, buses are plentiful and inexpensive, although the service is less frequent in the evening. There are two bus stations at Port Louis, one linking it with the north and the other with the plateau towns of Beau Bassin, Rose Hill,

Quatre Bornes and Curepipe in the south. Some of the older buses do not inspire confidence although many are being replaced by new models. Bus stops are identifiable by white lettering on a black background. Queues are orderly and tickets are purchased from the conductor. Buses are particularly crowded 8-9am and 4-5pm during the week. Stop bells are located at each seat. Ticket information offices are found at main bus stations.

By Car

Car Hire Companies
Avis
Al-Madina Street
Port Louis
☎ 208 1624

Beach Car Limited
Marcellement Swan
Pereybère
☎ 263 8239

Budget Car
Grand Gaube
☎ 263 8937

Europcar
Pailles
☎ 208 6054

Hertz Maurtourco
Royal Road
Curepipe
☎ 675 1453

Mask Touring Company
Ground floor of Gold Crest Hotel
St Jean Road
Quatre Bornes
☎ 454 6975

There are additional charges for insurance and collision damage.

Emergencies
The conditions of contract are shown on the hire vehicle documents which should be kept in the vehicle at all times. In cases of breakdown contact should be made with the hirer of the vehicle. Tyre punctures can be quickly and easily repaired for a few rupees at any garage. The police should attend any personal injury accidents and where damage only is involved it is sufficient to exchange names and addresses. In any event, the hirers of the vehicle should be informed. In cases of doubt or difficulty, call the police.

Documents Needed
Drivers should be over 23 and in possession of an international driving licence.

Driving Conditions
Mauritians refer to the 'motorway' between Port Louis and Plaisance. By European standards it is a trunk road, but for the purpose of this book, the term 'motorway' has been used.

Most of the roads are surfaced (some better than others) and if driving, especially at night, through the sugar cane areas, do watch out for deep gulleys on either side of the road. Names of towns and villages may appear in either French or English and can be poorly sited or concealed between sugar cane. Distances and speed limits are shown in either kilometres or miles, rarely both, andoften not at all.

There is a strong presence of traffic police, particularly on the Port Louis-Plaisance motorway. Tourists are rarely troubled by them and they are helpful when seeking their assistance.

Fuel
Fuel stations are open every day including Sundays and are manned by pump attendants. Two grades of petrol, regular and super, are available. Credit cards and cheques are not generally accepted.

Motoring Rules and Regulations
Hire cars are fitted with seat belts but the wearing of them is not compulsory. The wearing of crash helmets is not compulsory for motorcycles of less than 49cc. In Mauritius motorists drive on the left hand side of the road. Speed limits are 80kph (50mph) on motorways and 50kph (31mph) elsewhere. Seatbelts are not compulsary and there is no age restriction for front seat passengers.

By Taxi
Taxis, particularly those operating in the towns, are in poor condition. They are recognisable by black registration numbers on white plates. Their use should really be restricted for short journeys within the towns as they can be expensive and the fare depends upon the whims of the driver. They are meterless so agree upon the fare before commencing a journey. Any price quoted includes the return fare to the taxi stand. The official tariff, should be displayed inside the vehicle, with waiting time chargeable for the first 15 minutes and every additional 15 minutes. Drivers do not expect to be tipped.

Taxi drivers rarely adhere to their rates and any complaints should be made to the Mauritius Government Tourist Office or the National Transport Authority, Victoria Square, in Port Louis, quoting the number plate, driver's name and details of the journey.

For longer journeys it may be more economical to hire a taxi for the day and fix a price which should be less than a day's car hire. If you are lucky to find a knowledgeable taxi driver who can act as a guide try to keep his custom by using him regularly.

Licensed 'taxi trains' or shared taxis, operate near bus stops in some towns and villages. They cover a prescribed route and the fare is divided between the number of passengers. The taxis are dilapidated and overloaded but travelling this way can be cheap, fun and fast with fares working out to not much more than the official bus fare.

Weddings and Honeymoons

Mauritius is an ideal honeymoon destination. Foreign couples wishing to get married can now do so following changes in the Civil Status Act which repealed the statutory residency requirements.

The wedding is a civil legal ceremony and similar in style to that performed at a Register Office. The ceremony, in English, normally takes place on the beach at selected hotels and is presided over by the Island Registrar. The hotel management provides interpreters in cases of language difficulties and deals with paperwork and any local problems.

Weddings can be performed from Monday to Friday, excluding public holidays, and depend also on the commitments of the Registrar. Details of tour operators specialising in weddings and honeymoons can be obtained from the Mauritius Government Tourist Office.

Prior to travel, tour operators will need copies of the first six pages of both passports and both birth certificates which are forwarded to the authorities for processing in Mauritius. Documentary evidence is required in cases of divorce, change of name or where one or both parties are widowed.

The mechanics of getting married are quite simple. Having arrived at the hotel, arrangements are made to swear the original documents at the Supreme Court in Port Louis and a date is fixed with the Registrar.

For further information contact:
Registrar of Civil Status
 7th level
Emmanuel Anquetil Building
Port Louis
☎ (230) 201 1727

Index

Accommodation 171
Albion 80
Anse aux Anglais 138
Anse Jonchée 57
Arsenal 38

Baie aux Huîtres 139
Baie aux Tortues 37–38
Baie du Cap 67
Baie du Tombeau 38–40
Bambou Mountains 50, 54, 56, 57
Bambous (village) 80
Banks 171
Bassin Blanc 69
Bassin de la Paix 161
Beau Bassin 113–114, 127
  Balfour Gardens 113–114, 127
Beau Champ 68
Bel Ombre 67
Bell Village 105, 107
  African Cultural Centre 105, 107
  Alliance Francaise 105, 107
  China Cultural Centre 105, 107
Belle Mare 54
Black River (Rivière Noire) area 83, 89
Black River Gorges 124, 125
Blanche Mountains 50
Blue Bay 62
Bois Blanc 162
Bois Court 152

Bois des Amourettes 58
Boucan Canot 167
Bras Sec 157
Bras-Panon 160, 169, 170
Britannia Sugar Estate 75, 76

Cambuston 160
Camera Equipment 172
Candos Hill 119
Cap Malheureux 43–44
Cascade Niagara 160
Casela Bird Park 81–82, 89
Caverne Patate 142–143
Caverne Provert 138
Centre de Flacq 50–52, 64
Chamarel 86, 89
Champs de Mars 101
Chaudron 169
Chemin Grenier 69
Chemists 173
Cilaos 155, 156, 170
Cirques (Reunion) 153
Climate 176
Coin de Mire 48
Communications 174
Creole Mountains 50
Curepipe 120–124, 127
  Botanical Gardens 123–124, 127
  Royal College 121
Currency and Credit Cards 175

Customs Regulations 175

Deux Frères 56
Disabled (Facilites for) 178
Domaine du Chasseur 57–58
Domaine les Pailles 105, 107
Drink 17

East Coast 50-64
Electricity 176
Embassies 176
Emergencies 177
Entertainment 17
Etang-Salé (forest) 164, 169

Ferney 58
Festivals 178
Flat Island 48
Flic en Flac 80–81, 89
Flora and Fauna 18
Floreal 128
Food 17
Formica Léo 152
Frederica 68

Gabriel Island 48
Goodlands 44, 49
Grand Baie 41–43, 49, 138
Grand Bassin 125
Grand Gaube 44
Grand River South East 56
Grand Rivière Noire (river) 83
Grand Rivière Noire

189

(village) 84–85
Grand Sable 57
Grande Case Noyale 85
Grande Montagne 140
Grotte des Premiers
    Francais 167

Hell-Bourg 155, 169
Henrietta 127, 128
High Commissions
    176
History 9
Holidays (National)
    180

Île aux Aigrettes 62
Île aux Cerfs 55–56
Île aux Oiseau 57
Île aux Sables 144
Île Cocos 144
Île d'Ambre 44
Ilet à Cordes 157
Ilet Bethléem 161
Illness and Injury 178
Îlot Flamants 57
Insurance 181

Kanaka Crater 125

La Crete 85
La Ferme 143
La Gaulette 89
Là Mangue 143
La Mivoie 84
La Nicolière Reservoir
    47
La Plaine des
    Palmistes 170
La Preneuse 84
La Ravine Blanche 163
La Rivière 156
La Saline les Bains 165
Language 179
Le Cap Méchant 163
Le Gris Gris 72
Le Morne (village) 88
Le Morne Brabant
    (mountain) 88
Le Morne Peninsula
    88

Le Palmiste Rouge 156
Le Pavillion 156
Le Pétrin 125
Le Réduit 114
    Château 114–116
Le Souffleur 75
Le Tampon 153
Le Val Nature Park
    62–64
L'Echo 151
Legal Advice 180
Les Avirons 164
Les Makes 164
L'Étang-Salé Les Bains
    164
Local Events 178

Mafatte 157
Magenta Dam 82
Mahebourg 59, 60–62,
    64
    Historical and
    Naval Museum
    61–62, 64
Maïdo 157, 158
Mapou 47
Maps 180
Mare Longue 163
Mare Longue
    Reservoir 126
Marie Reine de la Paix
    102
Marine Life 25
Measurements 180
Medical Cover 181
Moka (region) 116,
    128
    Eureka House 116–
    117, 128
    Mahatma Gandhi
    Institute 116, 128
Moka Range (moun-
    tains) 90, 101, 103,
    105, 117
Mon Choisy 40, 49
Mont Blanc Reservoir
    71
Mont Lubin 140, 145

Mountains 24

Nez de Boeuf 151

Palissades 140, 145
Palmar 54
Pamplemousses 45–
    47, 49
    Royal Botanical
    Gardens 45–46, 49
Pas de Bellecombe 152
Passports 181
Pastimes 182
People and Culture 26
Pereybèrè 43
Petit Gabriel 142
Petit Sable 57
Petite Case Noyale 85
Petite Rivière 79
Petite Rivière Noire
    (river) 85
Phoenix 120, 128
Pieter Both (moun-
    tain) 117
Piton de la Fournaise
    (volcano) 149, 151-
    153
Piton des Neiges 149
Plaine Champagne
    124, 125–126
Plaine des Cafres 152
Plaine Magnien 75
Plaisance 75
Plateau Towns 109-
    128
Pointe aux
    Canonniers 41
Pointe aux Roches 68–
    69
Pointe aux Sables 77–
    79
Pointe Bernache 44
Pointe Canon 139
Pointe Cotton 141
Pointe du Bourbier
    161
Pointe Marcellin 163
Pomponnette 69

Index • 191

Port Louis 90-108
  Amicale Casino 99, 107
  Central Market 99
  Chinese Pagoda 103
  Chinese Quarter 99
  Church and Shrine of Père Laval 104–105
  Church of the Immaculate Conception 103
  City Hall 96, 107
  Company Gardens 95–96, 107
  Episcopal Palace 104
  General Post Office 100
  Government House 93
  Jummah Mosque 100
  Kwan Tee Temple 103
  La Citadelle 102, 107
  Line Barracks 101
  Mauritius Institute 94, 107
  Merchant Navy Club 100
  National Library 95
  Natural History Museum 94–95, 107
  Père Laval Museum 105, 107
  Place d'Armes 93
  Robert Edward Hart Gardens 105
  St James Cathedral 104
  St Louis Cathedral 103–104
  St Sacrament Church of Cassis 105
  SSR Memorial Centre for Culture 97, 107
  Theatre 96
  Treasury Buildings 94
  Western Cemetery 105

Port Louis (North of) 33-49
Port Mathurin 134–138, 145
Poudre d'Or 44–45
Puits des Anglais 163

Quartier Français 160
Quatre Bornes 117–119, 128
Quatre Cocos 53–54
Quatre Soeurs 56
Quatre Vents 142

Religion 181
Reunion 146-170
Riche en Eau 62
Rivière des Anguilles 73, 76
  La Vanille Croco-dile Park 73, 76
Rochester Falls 71
Rodrigues 129-145
Rose Hill 111–113, 128
  Arab Town 112
  Craft-Aid 111, 128
  Max Moutia Museum 111, 128
  Pharmacy 112-113
  Plaza Theatre 111
  Town Hall 111, 128
Round Island 48

Saint Gabriel 142
Salazie 153, 170
Savanne Mountains 69, 71
Shopping 182
Signal Mountain 102
Solitude 140

Souillac 71–72, 76
South Coast 65-76
Sports 182
St André 153, 160, 170
St Benoit 161, 170
St Denis 159, 167–169, 169, 170
St Gilles les Bains 165, 170
St Joseph 162, 163
St Leu 163, 165, 170
St Louis 155, 164
St Paul 157, 165, 167, 170
St Philippe 162–163
St Pierre 163, 170
Ste Anne 161
Ste Marie 159
Ste Rose 159, 162
Ste Suzanne 159–160
Surinam 71

Tamarin 82–83
Tamarin Falls 127
Toilets 181
Tombeau Bay 38
Tourist Information Centres 184
Travel 184
Trèfles 140
Triolet 40
Trou aux Biches 33
Trou d'Eau Douce 54
Tyack 73, 76

Vacoas 119
Val Riche Forest 67–68
Vieux Grand Port 58
Ville Noire 60
Visas 181
Voile de la Mariée 155

Weddings and Honeymoons 188
West Coast 77-89
Wildlife 145

Visitor's Guides
Tour & Explore with MPC Visitor's Guides

Austria
Austria: Tyrol &
    Vorarlberg
Britain:
Cornwall & Isles of
    Scilly
Cotswolds
Devon
East Anglia
Guernsey, Alderney
    and Sark
Hampshire & the
    Isle of Wight
Denmark
Jersey
Kent
Lake District
Scotland: Lowlands
Somerset, Dorset &
    Wiltshire
North Wales and
    Snowdonia
North York Moors,
    York & Coast
Northumbria
Northern Ireland
Peak District
Sussex
Yorkshire Dales &
    North Pennines

Crete
Egypt
Finland
Florida
France:
Alps & Jura
Corsica
Dordogne
Loire
Massif Central
Normandy Landing
    Beaches
Provence & Côte
    d'Azur
Germany:
Bavaria
Black Forest
Rhine & Mosel
Southern Germany
Iceland
Italy:
Florence & Tuscany
Italian Lakes
Northern Italy
Mauritius,
    Rodrigues &
    Reunion
Peru

Spain:
Costa Brava to Costa
    Blanca
Mallorca, Menorca,
    Ibiza &
    Formentera
Northern & Central
    Spain
Southern Spain &
    Costa del Sol
Sweden
Switzerland
Tenerife
Turkey
Yugoslavia: The
    Adriatic Coast

World Traveller
*The new larger format
Visitor's Guides*

Belgium & Luxem-
    bourg
Czechoslovakia
France
Holland
Norway
Portugal
USA

**A complete catalogue of all our travel guides to over
125 destinations is available on request**